THE WORKING COUNTRYSIDE 1862–1945

THE WORKING COUNTRYSIDE
1862–1945

ROBIN HILL AND PAUL STAMPER

SWAN·HILL
PRESS

Copyright © 1993 by Robin Hill and Paul Stamper

First published in the UK in 1993
by Swan Hill Press
Reprinted 1997

A catalogue record for this book
is available from the British Library

ISBN 1 85310 305 5

Printed in Hong Kong

Swan Hill Press
an imprint of Airlife Publishing Ltd
101 Longden Road, Shrewsbury SY3 9EB, England

CONTENTS

ACKNOWLEDGEMENTS

Our main debt is to all those people who so willingly loaned us their photographs for copying. Those who supplied photographs that are reproduced here are thanked below; we are equally grateful to all those whose photographs were copied but not, ultimately, used. All the photographs copied form a valuable addition to Shropshire's archival heritage, in the custody of Shropshire County Council's Records and Research Unit. We would also like to acknowledge the help of many other people, too numerous to mention individually, who acted as intermediaries, drawing photographs to our attention and, not infrequently, bringing them to us for us to copy. Theirs was an invaluable contribution.

The majority of the plates were printed by Vine Williams; the great care he took with often unprepossessing copy negatives deserves special mention. A good deal of the text was typed by Sue Ball; she too is thanked.

Acton Scott Historic Working Farm Plates 31, 42, 73, 92, 96, 97, 100, 101, 118, 126; Margaret Alderson 55, 56, 68, 69, 84, 94; the late Mrs P. E. Bird 138; Mr R. Blakeway 80, 99; Mrs D. Bourne 90; Mr Bradshaw 72; Lady Jennifer Brown 1, 6, 11, 22, 62, 83, 134, 136; Mr J. H. Bury 14, 15; Jean Chaplin 88; Mrs J. Chatham 4, 53; Clun Museum 2; Mrs M. Crawford Clarke 52, 87; Mrs B. Dale 76; B. and J. Davies, Bucknell 112, 119, 120, 121, 122, 125; Mr N. O. Edwards 78, 91; Mrs H. M. Evans 79; Miss S. J. Franklin 30, 38; Mr D. George 29; Mr E. Gill 17; Mrs J. Griffiths 57; Mr H. Hand 41, 44, 117; Harper Adams Agricultural College 105, 109, 115; Miss A. Hockenhull 93; Institute of Agricultural History & Museum of English Rural Life 16; Ironbridge Gorge Museum Trust 60; Mrs D. Jones 8; Mr E. Kinnish 81; Mr P. Klein 43; Lady Labouchere 40, 46, 47, 48, 49, 50, 67; Mr T. H. Leath 26; Jean Lindsay 37; Mrs F. M. Link 66; Ludlow Museum 27, 70, 70, 75; McCartneys, Auctioneers, of Ludlow 98; Mrs P. Milman 33; Mr R. K. Moore 35, 89; Mr J. W. Morris 20, 21; Much Wenlock Museum 123, 139; Pentabus Project 10, 12, 61, 65, 85, 131, 132, 133, 140; Mr R. H. C. Phillips 142; Mr F. Powell 107, 137; Miss M. I. Powell 106, 108; Mr T. Pryce 51; Miss M. Puckle 86; Miss U. Rayska 24; Dr D. H. Robinson 7, 18, 65, 141; Shropshire Records and Research Unit 5, 19 23, 25, 28, 36, 39, 45, 71, 103, 104, 144; Mrs P. Stones 135; Times Newspapers 102; Mr S. M. Turner 9, 64; Mrs M. W. Uttley 127, 128, 129; Mrs J. Ward 13, 114, 124; Wellington Journal and Shrewsbury News 143; Whitchurch Area Archaeological Group 34; Mrs J. Williams 32, 58, 130; Mr and Mrs G. Wright 3, 54, 59, 110, 111, 113; Mrs J. Yates 116.

INTRODUCTION

The broad theme of this book is work in the Shropshire countryside from the advent of photography to the end of the Second World War and, more specifically, work in agriculture and the rural crafts. From the outset it was decided to exclude major industrial enterprises which happened, usually because of the location of raw materials, to lie in the countryside. Thus work in collieries, quarries, clay and brick works, and potteries is unrepresented here. Also excluded were members of the professions, notably clergymen and school teachers. Likewise a number of activities which we determined were engaged in for pleasure, rather than of necessity or for a wage, were omitted from the collection; thus the gamekeeper appears but not the sporting gunman, the blacksmith but not the huntsman.

The book has its origins in picture research for *The Victoria History of Shropshire*, Volume IV, *Agriculture* (1989), and its popular abridgement *'The Farmer Feeds Us All': A Short History of Shropshire Agriculture* (1989). It was found that the public photographic archives, principally those of Shropshire County Council's Records and Research Unit (which brought together the County Record Office and the Shrewsbury Local Studies Library), had very few old agricultural photographs. Thus a series of appeals was made, both publicly and via contacts in the farming world, and gradually a collection was assembled, a part of which was published in the above-mentioned volumes.

Many interesting photographs had, however, to be excluded on the grounds of space. It seemed a great pity to consign these, unseen, to the archive, especially as there was clearly present the core of a collection which had some claim, given the subject matter and geographical coverage, to be considered as a representative and useful body of source material. It was at that stage that the concept of the present book was outlined: a thematically arranged collection of pre-1945 photographs from Shropshire, with commentaries on the material which by the standards of many 'old photograph' books might be considered as extended. Once the parameters had been set, the search for material continued, especially where the existing coverage of subjects which we wished to include was poor or entirely lacking.

Inevitably, even given the best efforts of the authors and the many people who made a great contribution by acting almost as local correspondents, searching out material from friends, neighbours, and relatives, some activities remain poorly or completely unrepresented. There is no photograph here, for instance, of an early mechanical milking parlour, nor of beekeeping, nor of many of the specialist rural crafts which were carried on in Shropshire. In the last category one thinks of brewing, chair bodging, and besom and basket making, and that is confining oneself only to the second letter of the alphabet. It may well be that publication of this book brings some of this material to light; if so, one of our aims will have been fulfilled.

Few of the photographs reproduced in this book could be rated, either in technical accomplishment or artistic content, as above average for their time. Many were taken as snapshots, with no thought of posterity. That should not suprise us, for documentary photography, where the photographer seeks to record proficiently yet without sentimentality the ordinary, mundane, and often un-attractive, has always been a minor interest.

Many of the better photographs, in terms of technical quality, were taken by professionals, of which the county had at least twenty by 1870. The bulk of their work was portraiture, mostly undertaken in studios using fixed props, painted backgrounds, and often artificial lighting. Occasionally, however, especially where there was the prospect of producing multiple sets of prints with a postcard format, photographers ventured forth into the less controlled environment of the outside world to work. Even so, not least because of the use of heavy, tripod-mounted field cameras, and the continued requirement for relatively long exposures and thus static subjects, photographers tended to concentrate on formal group compositions, such as haymakers.

However, the most interesting photographs encountered in the research for this book, where a documentary approach has been taken (whether consciously or not) and often the different stages of a process illustrated in successive images, tended to be those taken by amateurs. Of these several were women. Lilla Haughton Buddicom (d. 1914), for instance, the daughter of a minor landowner, apparently took up photography in 1866 when about twenty-two years old. She had a good camera, an excellent eye for composition, and unusually took as many pictures of cottages and cows (see, for example, plates 1, 6, 62 and 81) as she did of her family and friends. She continued to take photographs until about 1893, and her albums are a unique record of life in the second half of the nineteenth century in and around the south Shropshire village of Ticklerton. Perhaps the most accomplished amateur photographer, as equally at home with a cine camera as a still one, was Frances Pitt (d. 1964), who became well known as a writer on natural history. In her autobiography she recalled how her interest in photography had been kindled, and how over the years her equipment had been upgraded from a Brownie, purchased for 5s. in 1900, to a technically more advanced 'Frena', then to a Thornton-Pickard, a folding field camera. A Leica, the first and always one of the finest 35 mm cameras, was later among her equipment. Among photographs taken with the 'Frena' were series taken in 1907 and 1909 showing haymaking and harvesting (plates 40, 46–50), subjects she was to return to about 1940 with her cine camera, loaded with some of the first colour stock. Mention should also be made of the quite unique series of photographs (of which plate 140 is one) taken by the seventeen year old May Jordan in 1934 of her grandfather and great-uncle, Wellington's last bowl turners, with her box Brownie camera, newly purchased for 8s.4d.

Most of the copy photography for this book was done using a 35 mm Minolta XXX (frequently with extension tubes) loaded with Ilford Pan F or a Mamiya C 330 loaded with a variety of slow films. Prints, negatives, and film record sheets generated in the course of research for this book have been deposited with Shropshire County Council's Records and Research Unit.

What, above all else, determined what agricultural regimes were possible in Shropshire were its physical characteristics. South and west of the Severn, which flows south-eastwards across the county, are uplands, a land of hills, ridges and dales. By contrast, east and north of the Severn are wide, rolling plains which extend off into Staffordshire and Cheshire, interrupted only occasionally by sandstone hills.

Within those two broad divisions a number of 'agricultural regions' can be defined, partly on the basis of geology and relief but also taking into account soils, climate, vegetation and drainage. The *Victoria History of Shropshire* IV (1989) isolated eight such regions, from the 'North-West Uplands' west of Oswestry to the 'Clee Hills Plateau' in the south-east of the county and the 'Eastern Sandstone Plain' east of Bridgnorth. Within these may be found smaller sub-regions — landscapes with particular soils or characteristics — such as the weald moors to the west of Newport or the Teme valley south of Ludlow and Cleobury Mortimer. Even within these, as the working countryman would be aware, a wide diversity of conditions may prevail, all of which must be taken into account when decisions are made about land use and farming practices. Today, and far more so in the past, farmers can only do what the land will allow.

The mid nineteenth century was an unusually buoyant period for British agriculture. Worries that the 1846 repeal of the Corn Laws would encourage large-scale cereal imports and so depress the country's farming sector had proved groundless. After a brief uncertainty, the price of wheat — the usual barometer of agriculture's prosperity — soon steadied to usher in a golden age of development and productivity.

Several significant steps had already been taken that were to help spread the news of agricultural improvement. The Royal Agricultural Society, founded in 1838, published a regular and informative journal and organised annual peripatetic shows, and this together with the London-based Farmers' Club (1844), provided a model for several local agricultural societies within Shropshire.

A more formal agricultural education was to be obtained at the Royal College of Agriculture, started at Cirencester in 1845 by a group of landowners.

Many of the technical and scientific improvements of the period were to influence agriculture until the middle of the twentieth century. Labour-saving machines began to appear on the land, particularly at harvest-time. These mowers, tedders, rakes and reapers, typical products of Victorian ingenuity, were mass-produced and distributed throughout the country on an expanding rail network. The use of steam was soon transferred from the railways to the farmyard, where engines were used for ploughing, threshing and processing crops.

The invention of efficient tile-making machines in the 1840s enabled the underdrainage of thousands of acres of wet and marginal land. Once drained such ground was then able to fully benefit from the scientific advances that produced superphosphates and the improved sea communications that brought Chilean nitrates, Peruvian guano and German potash to fertilise British soils.

Such advances in agriculture enabled output to rise to satisfy the demands of a growing urban population. When a series of cold wet years curtailed this expansion in the mid 1870s consumers were forced to look elsewhere for sufficient supplies of cereals. The lifting of import restrictions thirty years previously meant that wheat from the North American prairies and the Russian steppes began to replace home-grown crops, and as the poor harvests continued this trade accelerated. Imports of grain more than doubled in the twenty years after 1870, market prices were halved, and many British farmers were left in a precarious position.

It was on the arable farms of eastern England that these changes were felt most keenly. Livestock farmers, however, were experiencing a similar downturn in their fortunes. In a pre-veterinary age cattle plague and liver rot in sheep were a scourge during the 1870s, and outbreaks of foot and mouth disease in the early 1880s severely reduced the size of the national flock. Overseas competition was also being felt, particularly by sheep farmers. The introduction of continuous refridgeration in the holds of ever-faster steamships enabled New Zealand lamb and mutton to compete with the cheaper home produced cuts. By 1895 meat imports were supplying about one-third of the market.

The lean years of the final quarter of the nineteenth century forced most farmers to re-examine their practices. Many cereal growers who had relied upon wheat for their income now planted barley and oats as these still found a good market as animal feed. Others gave up corn in favour of livestock rearing, and in the period 1870–1900 the area of grassland in the country increased by four million acres. A significant number chose not to leave arable enterprises completely but to move into market gardening. This option made sound sense for farmers near large urban centres, and the recorded area of market gardens more than doubled between 1875 and 1895.

Adjustments were also made by the more perceptive livestock farmer. He saw that he was unable to undercut cheap imports and chose instead to concentrate on producing high quality meat and dairy products. The supply of fresh milk to urban centres became an option for those close to rail links, and the establishment of local creameries — like the one at Minsterley, Shropshire — gave an outlet to others. For the specialist breeder of livestock the growing overseas demand gave British agriculture a rare export opportunity in these troubled years.

For agricultural labourers the period of depression worsened their already-difficult position. As a class they had to endure the persistent problems of low wages, the threat of redundancy in the face of increasing mechanisation, and often squalid housing.

Average wages in Shropshire were about 12s.3d. a week in 1869, with the possibility of some farm produce as a 'perk'. It was in response to such low wages that a local farm labourers' union was established in south Shropshire in 1871 and the National Agricultural Labourers' Union in the following year. But the difficulties of organising such a dispersed workforce meant that this trade unionism was only partially successful. Many farm workers left the countryside for the towns, and the number of men employed in the industry was halved during the second half of the nineteenth century. For those remaining on farms their accommodation was usually rudimentary and cramped.

Where living conditions for labourers were above the average then it was sometimes due to the efforts of land-owners — such as the Duke of Sutherland and the Leightons of Loton — in building improved accommodation. Shropshire was a county where in the mid-Victorian years over half of the land was owned by large estates of 3,000 acres or more. Such landowners not only took an interest in the labourers on their estates but also involved themselves with their farming tenants. Many gave financial and practical assistance to the farmers on their estates to help them through the worst of the late nineteenth-century depression. Rent reductions of between fifteen and twenty per cent were common in Shropshire, with much higher figures recorded in eastern England as landlords endeavoured to keep their farms tenanted and cultivated. However, some landowners joined the farmers and labourers as victims of the continuing depression and were forced to part with property.

Following a brief period of relative prosperity during the First World War, when the need for home-produced foodstuffs gave farmers a better market, agriculture returned to poorer times in the 1920s. Numbers of large estates within the county were sold by owners who could not afford to run them but who saw some salvation in the higher prices of an improved property market. Whilst such sales gave tenants the opportunity to purchase their own farms — owner-occupation of farms in the county increased from eight per cent in 1911 to eighteen per cent in 1922 and to thirty per cent by 1941 — it also left large areas of the countryside without the paternalistic influence of a large landowner who could assist in times of hardship or need.

An uninspiring time for agriculture, the inter-war years did bring several new opportunities for the farmer. With the decline in the cultivation of traditional root crops — mangolds, swedes and turnips — came the new cash crop of sugar beet. Introduced into Shropshire in 1922, the crop brought additional benefits to growers both from a government subsidy and via the building of a processing factory at Allscott in 1927. Also during the 1920s the county established a reputation for the production and sale of farmhouse cheese, and despite the ready market for liquid milk following the formation of the Milk Marketing Board in 1933 this activity persisted until the onset of the Second World War. A further government initiative — the Wheat Act of 1932 — provided incentives that doubled the area of the county under wheat in four years.

With the onset of war in 1939 the pace of change in the countryside again quickened. Government subsidies, aimed at increasing the home-grown food supply, encouraged Shropshire farmers to plough up 40,000 acres of grassland in the year from May 1939. Additional cultivation on this scale led to increased mechanisation, particularly in the form of tractor-power but with new drills and root harvesters also making timely appearances. With a reduced labour force such mechanical and time-saving equipment was becoming essential. Even when peace returned farming did not resume many of its time-honoured ways; agriculture had taken a major stride forward into the modern age.

Opposite:

1 Thomas Goodman, 1881

Thomas Goodman was 81 when this photograph was taken. He then lived at Heywood, near Ticklerton, with his daughter, son-in-law, three grandchildren, and step-daughter.

Born at Wistanstow, a few miles to the south-west, in the reign of George III, Goodman would have seen great changes in agricultural practice during his lifetime. Draught oxen had finally given way to horses, steam powered machinery had become commonplace, and many new breeds had appeared such as Hereford and Shorthorn cattle and Shropshire sheep.

The trade directories of the time describe him as a farmer but the 1881 census enumerators, probably more accurately, put him down as an agricultural labourer. Whatever, Goodman's smock immediately marked him as someone who worked on the land. Smocks differed from region to region and his, with its heavy protective over-collar, was typical of that worn in south Shropshire and the adjoining areas. Often men had two smocks: for work a plain one, soaked in linseed oil to make it waterproof, and for Sunday an elaborately decorated or 'smocked' one such as Goodman is wearing here.

In the thirty years preceding 1881 the smock, or 'slop frock', had mostly fallen from favour, and it was mainly old men like Goodman that still wore them. Around Ford smocks were still worn in the 1870s, but a Mr Swain of Ryton (in Condover), who died about 1895, was reckoned to be the last to. Similarly in Childs Ercall the last smock-wearer was reckoned to be James Beard, a farm labourer, in the years around 1880. He was later remembered as having taken just one day's holiday a year, in the autumn after harvest, in order to visit Market Drayton's Dirty Fair. Here he would bank his savings, and buy a new frock for his wife and a new smock for himself.

1 The Country Population

In the main, the farm labourer's lot in late nineteenth and early twentieth-century Shropshire was unenviable, even by the standards of the time. Wages were low, and the county's cottages were infamously bad: tumbledown, leaky, and with too few bedrooms. That was especially so in the Clun area, and in 1869 an observer reckoned the housing there 'deplorable' and worse even than Dorset's, then generally regarded as the country's poorest. Part of the trouble was that the demand for cottages had increased as the number of farm labourers 'living in', that is residing in the employer's farmhouse, had declined from about forty *per cent* in 1861 to sixteen *per cent* in 1871.

Little improved for labourers as the century wore on, while material expectations rose and opportunities outside agriculture, especially in towns, increased. And if landowners and farmers had generally done well out of farming in the previous generation, the great depression in agriculture which began in the mid 1870s hit them hard. The numbers engaged in agriculture in Shropshire fell, from 21,165 labourers and 6,102 farmers in 1871 to 13,497 and 5,543 repectively in 1911. By about the turn of the century farmers were becoming concerned by the shortage of labour.

However, as much in the earlier twentieth century as in the previous decades, the life of the farm labourer was one to be avoided if alternatives were available. Cottages remained generally poor during the inter-war years, the low quality of accommodation hardly being compensated for by the low rents asked. Despite low rents balancing the weekly budget was difficult, especially for those with several dependent children. Even such basics as children's shoes might only be afforded if the wife undertook seasonal work such as potato and beet lifting.

2   George and Mary Miles, about 1880

A marvellously evocative photograph of an elderly couple, George and Mary Miles, of Dudgeley Mill, All Stretton, wearing everyday country clothing of the mid nineteenth century.

His smock is heavily 'smocked' which suggests it is his Sunday best. Canvas leggings, heavy boots, billycock hat and a neckerchief complete the visible ensemble. Mrs Miles wears the usual dress of the female field worker: a heavy ankle-length skirt and a long white apron, a print blouse, and a sun bonnet, in fashion in the countryside between about 1840 and 1914. By 1880 only in the south-west Shropshire might full-time female agricultural workers still have been found outside the dairy, most parts of the county having seen an end to their employment between about 1830 and 1860. Nevertheless, for decades afterwards women continued to be taken on as casual workers in the summer, especially at harvest time.

3 Jack Buckley, summer 1914

As the British Expeditionary Force was in retreat after Mons, Jack Buckley was busy at Espley, near Cound, with the wheat harvest. The field is a large one, and its seems likely that he was scything out the headland in order to give access to the horse-drawn reaper. His clothing is typical for the time: heavy trousers gathered below the knee, a flannel shirt, waistcoat, neckerchief, and flat cap.

4   An Irish gang, Linley, early twentieth century
This nine-strong harvest gang stooking barley at Linley farm, near Broseley, were probably among the many migrants who crossed the Irish Sea each year to do seasonal farm work. They seem to be binding the crop by hand, an unpleasant task and the reason for the protective sacking aprons.

The owner of the photograph recalls how his father, born in 1872, told him how gangs would come from Ireland early in the year to plant potatoes, staying on successively to hoe mangolds and swedes, harvest the hay and corn, finally to return home after lifting the potato crop. Each gang had a leader who would go from farm to farm to seek out work and negotiate wages. On many farms such gangs were known as 'moaners' because of their reaction if they found no work was available, or the conditions not to their liking.

The annual Irish migration was probably at its peak in the 1870s and 1880s, and by the time the photograph was taken the number coming over each year was falling. It came to an end with the First World War.

5   A harvest gang, Ness Strange, about 1887

A group of labourers photographed in a rick yard during a meal break. Copious quantities of drink — whether beer, cider, or cold tea — were very much a necessity at harvest time, and flagons and jugs appear in many of the photographs in this book. Rarely, however, were they as elaborate as those seen here.

The thick clothes and heavy studded boots were the typical everyday summer work-wear in the late nineteenth and early twentieth century. Although hot they afforded some protection from the sharp stalks of sheaves and stubble, against the irritating dust which flew off corn and hay as it was cut and carried, and in the case of the boots against a misplaced horse hoof. Just as much though it was convention that dictated, even to field gangs, that it was improper, perhaps even unhealthy, to work without a shirt or hat on. Shorts seem never to have been worn, or trousers rolled up.

6 George Williams, 1892

Williams was about fifty when photographed bringing a load of brushwood home to Soudley, near Eaton-under-Heywood. The stick may have been a concession to his wooden leg, one of the reasons, along with his bad temper, why the local children were frightened of him.

Old age and retirement, probably enforced by ill-health, were approached with at best apprehension and not infrequently dread by countrymen. During their working lives wages were generally so low that only the most provident managed to save a small nest egg for their old age. Even the most industrious labourers, if long lived, might end their days in the workhouses set up in 1836–7. Here conditions were harsh, husbands were separated from wives, and privileges few. Some found a home elsewhere: in the 1850s the commonest class of patient in Shropshire's county asylum consisted of those deranged by the 'ceaseless labours and anxieties of the lowest rank of labouring independence'.

7 Topping parsnips, Edgmond area, 1930s

Just how cold and monotonous winter jobs would be on the farm is graphically illustrated by this photograph. What no picture can fully reveal are the social and economic hardships endured by farmworkers and their families: low wages, poor housing, and what today we would call social deprivation.

At this time wages, which other than in the exceptional wartime years had been low since the onset of the great agricultural depression in the 1870s, were around thirty shillings for a 54-hour week. Union activity was slight, and the number of branches of the National Union of Agricultural Workers in Shropshire had fallen from 70 at the end of the First World War to just over 40 in 1931. While farm cottage rents were low, at about three shillings a week, much accommodation was of a deplorable standard and there was little rural housing provision by local authorities. Especially where couples had more than two children the family was likely to be ill-clothed and poorly shod. A wireless, bought on hire-purchase, was likely to be the family's only regular source of entertainment.

Opposite:

8   William Woolley, about 1940

Smallholders, who combine the farming of anything between two or three and twenty or thirty acres with other, paid, employment, have always been relatively numerous in Shropshire. William Woolley, who lived and worked at Wern Tanglas, near Newcastle in south-west Shropshire, was as typical as any of the smallholder class.

Born in the 1880s, he had his own smallholding where he lived with his wife and daughters and which he farmed part-time. The greater part of his income, however, came from his employment on a relative's farm. He is remembered as having been a competent and 'tidy' worker, and was a champion hedger.

Mr Woolley's clothing, if hardly stylish, is eminently practical for a stint of winter ploughing. Nevertheless, the sack belted around his waist would probably only put up a token defence against the hard and cold iron seat of the tractor.

9   Haymakers at Hinstock, early twentieth century

Haymaking was one of the main activities in the farming round when people 'pitched in' to get the job done as quickly as possible. That is likely to be the explanation for the elaborate, elegant, and freshly laundered Edwardian clothing of these three haymakers — and indeed, of many of the other women seen elsewhere in this book engaged in outdoor summer tasks. These were not true agricultural workers — that is women who of economic necessity spent weeks or months each year doing farm work — rather they were the farmer's wife, daughters, relatives, or servants.

10 Navvies and their families, Bucknell, about 1902

The Victorian countryside had a far more mobile population than we might imagine. The young, especially, often moved on an annual basis from one employer to another, and not infrequently this involved removing to a new community. Nevertheless most of the population movement remained within the locality, which thus saw only gradual change in its social composition and family networks.

Every now and then, however, the essential stability and balance of an area could be disrupted by the arrival of gangs employed on the massive civil engineering projects which were such a feature of the Victorian age. Steam powered machinery was available and was used, but even so a huge amount of work was done by hand.

Such was the case in the first years of the twentieth century when water was brought by pipe and conduit from the Elan valley in mid Wales to Birmingham. For three years three thousand navvies and their dependents were housed in huts in the station yard at Bucknell, outnumbering the inhabitants of the small village on the Shropshire-Herefordshire border by about ten to one.

11 Gypsies on the Whitcliffe, Ludlow, about 1889

Little, for sure, is known about the gypsies that moved through the county in the past. The occasional reference in a printed work, and the oral history of the gypsies themselves, suggests that families or groups tended to spend each year moving around the same general circuit. That might cover an area such as north Herefordshire and south Shropshire, with employment being found in successive agricultural tasks such as potato planting, hoeing, the hay and corn harvests, and fruit and hop picking. Money might also be earned by tin smithing — repairing pots and pans — in which many gypsies were skilled.

This excellent photo shows what appears to be a small family group camped overlooking Ludlow. The bender tents were used as living and sleeping accommodation; the 'classic' heavy, painted gypsy wagon only developed in the twentieth century. The vehicles in this photograph would have been used solely for carting about the family's possessions and, apparently, its stock of baskets for sale, just visible in the left-hand cart. One suspects that the boy in the incongruous deerstalker cap is the photographer's son.

12 Gypsies, Bucknell, early twentieth century
*An unposed group sitting by the ashes of the fire, over which are
the iron hooks from which the kettles and pan would have been
suspended. On the ground by the right-hand woman is a straw
boater which, like the baskets in the previous photograph, may
have been manufactured for sale.*

13 Gypsy girl, Much Wenlock, early twentieth century
This girl was photographed on the High Causeway, just outside Much Wenlock. She was leaving the town, presumably having gone there to sell items from her basket such as home-made pegs and sprigs of lavender.

2 Land Management

For land to be maintained in good heart there were many jobs that had to be done outside the more obvious round of ploughing, harvesting, and stock rearing. Buildings had to repaired, ditches cleared, hedges cut, gates mended, and vermin kept down. All required a regular, and on larger farms a considerable investment of labour, and thus money.

In 1881 the Shropshire Chamber of Agriculture complained that on many farms conditions of cleanliness and cultivation were 'defective'. No doubt money was becoming tighter as the depression in agriculture continued, but the largest single problem was the growing shortage of manpower. Over the previous decade education had become compulsory if not always free, and accordingly ever-fewer boys were available as cheap labour. At the same time there was an increasing drift from the land as families left the countryside to try their luck in towns.

As the depression continued the fabric of the countryside deteriorated still further. Obviously, the picture was different in each region and on every estate, but a net decline there undoubtedly was. That was exacerbated by a steady break up by sale of the great estates, the most visible sign of which was the demolition by 1950 of at least thirty-five of the county's ninety or so country houses standing in the 1890s. Less noticeably, the inter-war years saw all too many buildings, hedges and drains left unmaintained. During the same period the county council extended its activities to river and land drainage work, and launched campaigns against injurious weeds and vermin, but it could only do so much with the very limited funds available.

Opposite:

14   The keepers, Oakly Park, about 1912

From the mid eighteenth century increasing attention was paid to the preservation of game, and especially after about 1850 when landowners' worries about a possible repeal of the game laws began to lessen. The protection of rabbits, in particular, often brought landowners into conflict with their tenants, who had to stand by as their crops were destroyed. The Willey estate was probably the most highly preserved in the county, although the game also ran largely unchecked on many others, such as the Apley Park, Hawkstone, and Walcot estates. Sir Baldwin Leighton of Loton Park gained considerable notoriety in 1855 when he prosecuted his own gamekeeper for stealing a couple of rabbits.

The management of game and the enforcement of a strict game preservation policy required a large number of keepers. Here at Oakly Park, a moderate estate in south Shropshire and a seat of the Earl of Plymouth, the head keeper, Alexander Horsburgh (seated), apparently had ten under keepers to assist him. Such was the manpower, and on the part of the landlord the investment, behind the shooting parties of Edwardian England.

15 A vermin pole, Downton Hall, about 1928

Game preservation, the neglect of basic land maintenance during the hard times of the great agricultural depression of the 1870s and later, and the loss of farmworkers from the land during the First World War, all contributed to many areas being almost overrun by vermin in the post-war era. That fact is graphically illustrated by this photograph, taken on the Downton Hall estate, near Ludlow, in which magpies, hedgehogs, stoats and weasels are all hung in profusion.

Opposite:

16 A rabbit catcher, Exfords Green, about 1940

Robert Darlow of Woodbine Villa, Exfords Green, close to the foot of Lyth Hill, was ninety when this photograph was taken. A rabbit catcher, he is shown with the tools of his trade: gin traps and snares, a strong spade, and a terrier. The wheelbarrow to carry all his paraphernalia may have been a concession to his advancing years.

Rabbits have an interesting history. Introduced to England by the Normans, in the thirteenth century a rabbit cost more than a craftsman earned in a day. Gradually over the centuries rabbits became better adapted to the British climate, more numerous, and less expensive. By the nineteenth century they were sufficiently cheap to be a staple food of the poor, and in many areas were doing serious damage to crops. Where landlords permitted — and that was far from everywhere, with some landlords' attitudes to game preservation bordering on the fanatical — men like Darlow performed a vital service for the farmer. It was always a losing battle, however, and in 1953 the South American myxomatosis virus was introduced to the country. It killed 99 per cent of the rabbit population, and for a time it mistakenly looked as if the problem was solved.

17   A molecatcher, 1930s

Tom Hamlet, (d. 1940), seen here, and his brother Harry were molecatchers who lived in Norton-in-Hales. They would bicycle to jobs with their traps and their special short-handled narrow-bladed spades strapped to their bikes. As well as moles they trapped rats, stoats and other vermin, all of which were left hung on the barbed wire fence when the job was concluded.

Another Shropshire molecatcher, a Mr Hobdon, who worked the Whitchurch area between the wars, would call at farms twice a year. He was paid 1d. an acre, regardless of what was caught, and had the skins as a perk. The carcasses were left hung on a fence, usually near a gate, as proof of the number caught.

Opposite:

18 and 19   The musk rat trapper, about 1932

The musk rat, or musquash, was introduced to this country from Alaska in 1905. Despite the fact that these fast-breeding rodents were becoming a menace throughout central Europe musquash farms were started in both Scotland and England in 1927. By the early 1930s many animals had escaped, had established colonies in the wild, and were beginning to cause extensive damage burrowing into river banks, dams, and railway embankments.

In 1932 Shropshire County Council took on Brendan Vallings, who had experience in Canada as a trapper, to control the musk rats, in what was thought to be one of England's worst affected counties. Vallings used a Canadian canoe (carried about on top of a van) to float down rivers, especially the Severn, spotting signs of the animals. These included burrows and 'lodges', mounds of vegetation constructed as shelters and food stores. Once located, gassing and especially trapping were used to take the musk rats. The infestation, in fact, was less serious than imagined, and between 1932 and 1936 fewer than three thousand musk rats were exterminated in Shropshire. Even so, the campaign cost £10,000 and employed up to two dozen trappers at its peak.

20 and 21   Hedging, Pulverbatch, mid 1940s

A good thick hedge is a boundary rarely bettered. While fence posts rot, and wire rusts and eventually breaks, a well-managed hedge naturally replenishes itself. In the eighteenth and nineteenth centuries the majority of Shropshire's fields were bounded in this way. Most of its ancient fields were edged with a hedge and ditch, as were most of the new closes created as the old open fields and commons were inclosed from the fifteenth century onwards. Dry stone walls are to be found in the west and south of the county, especially dividing up the late-inclosed uplands, but most are hastily constructed, ramshackle affairs, far removed from those to be seen in the Peak district or the Yorkshire Dales.

It is now accepted that the older a hedge is the more the species it will contain. Many of Shropshire's most recent hedges, those of the eighteenth and nineteenth centuries, began life as bundles of thousands of quickthorn 'sets', supplied either by the estate or by one of the many commercial nurseries. Older hedges, some perhaps ribbons left as woodland was cleared, are far more species-rich. Especially notable are the impenetrable holly hedges of south Shropshire; are these remnants of long-gone ancient woodland, or have they been deliberately fostered because of the value of holly as browse?

If given a winter cut, traditionally with a long handled slasher or hook, a good hedge is likely to need very little maintenance. A neglected hedge, however, will soon grow tall and bushy, with gaps at its bottom through which stock can pass. Here more radical treatment, of laying, will be required. Having removed the branches shooting sideways and any uprights thought too heavy to lay, the hedger will proceed by making a cut with his billhook (or, in the case of thick material, his axe) close to the base of a stem, almost severing it. This stem is then bent over until nearly parallel with the ground. The hedger then proceeds to the next stem, which is treated likewise, being lain on to the top of the first. Stakes are driven into the hedge at intervals and the partially severed stems woven around these uprights to provide a living stock-proof barrier.

The hedger needs few tools beyond his billhook, axe and a thick, leather mitten with which to handle the thorny stems. It was always a winter job, done when the hedge was clear of summer leaf growth, as can be seen in these photographs showing Mr Jack Morris and a workman (with glove) laying a hedge on New House farm, Pulverbatch. It was probably a young hedge being laid for the first time.

22 Clearing gorse, Larden, 1905

Gorse, which is particularly associated with light, sandy soils, can be highly invasive unless managed. As here, a tall, dense, thorny scrub can grow up in just a few years. To clear it there are two options, burning and cutting. Often burning is favoured, not only because it is quick and easy, but also because the young shoots which readily regenerate from the burnt off old growth provide good grazing, especially for sheep, on what may otherwise be poor, thin pasture. Here concern that a fire might run out of control, threatening the adjoining woodland, may have been the reason for the gorse being cut. Gorse was often sold, bundled up in faggots, as it burns quickly with intense heat, which made it ideal for heating bread ovens.

23   Peat beds, Whixall Moss, about 1940

In past times peat was cut in many parts of north Shropshire and burnt as a fuel. Only this century did it begin to be used for horticultural purposes. In the nineteenth and twentieth centuries the principal peat cutting area was around Whixall, near Prees. The right to cut the 'turf', as the peat was known locally, technically a common right called turbary, was enjoyed by most families in the area who paid a small rent to the lord of the manor for it. Historically each of the commoners worked his own patch or 'bank', cutting peat, often on a part-time basis, between October and March. The peat was dug out in ditches or beds 44 yards long by two feet wide and three feet deep. Special tools had evolved to extract the wet, spongy peat, such as 'stickers' to mark out the shape of the blocks and 'uplifters' to remove them from the ground. Near the surface the peat was light coloured and of relatively poor quality, but darker peat, better for burning, lay beneath. Once cut the turves were stacked, ready to begin the long process of drying out over the summer before they could be sold.

On Whixall Moss a change in extraction methods came after the foundation in 1923 of the Midland Moss Litter Company's factory. Locally this was known as 'the Dutch firm', because it used Dutch methods of cutting and drying peat. Rather than the traditional local turf, the six inch by six inch by two inch 'Whixall Bible', the factory cut larger blocks, six inches by six inches by eighteen. Interestingly even those commoners who still cut peat for local distribution soon changed over to the new turf size.

By the 1920s new markets were opening up for the Moss's products. Some of the peat was going as litter to stables or to poultry farms using the deep litter method, and some as bulb fibre. There was also a thriving local cottage industry in making wreaths, using live moss together with holly and other appropriate foliage. Many of the wreaths went north to Lancashire, in 1954 one local agent (also a peat cutter) despatching four thousand of them.

Even in the 1980s one or two commoners still exercised their right to dig peat. In 1990, however, in the face of an intensification of commercial extraction, Whixall, Fenns, and Bettisfield Mosses were purchased by the Nature Conservancy Council, and peat extraction ceased.

Opposite:

24 Carrying peat, about 1900

The peat that was cut by the commoners found its market in the surrounding area. Most was probably distributed by cart but this photograph suggests more primitive methods were also seen. It may be that in some families there was a division of labour, with the man cutting the peat and his wife carrying and selling it. As fuel it was cheap but poor, giving out relatively little heat and producing a great deal of dusty ash.

25 A lengthsman, late nineteenth century

In 1888, probably about the time this photo was taken, the county council became responsible for the maintenance of Shropshire's 607 miles of roads and its bridges. Day-to-day road repair was carried out by local 'lengthsmen', each responsible for a mile or so of road. Pot holes and ruts were filled with dry stones, just visible in the wheelbarrow, to be ground in by passing traffic. The men worked largely unsupervised, and there were many complaints about the system's efficiency. Nevertheless, only in 1955 were the final lengthsmen retired.

26 Collecting water, Tugford, about 1900

Even in the country such a basic commodity as fresh water might not be close to hand. If the local geology was favourable it was possible for households to have a well or cistern, but this was far from universal. Elsewhere water had to be got from a nearby river, stream, or spring, and carriage of it was an irksome and all too regular task. Here, at Tugford Mill, water barrels are being filled at a spring. By this time a few villages were being provided with piped water, usually to communal pumps or taps, by philanthropic landlords, but these were very much in the minority. Only a generation later did local authorities begin to bring piped water to rural communities, a slow and expensive process. Tugford remained without mains water at the end of the Second World War, and even today not all villages are on the main.

Behind the water collectors a splendid dovecote can be seen. Presumably this was the miller's, the birds feeding off the waste grain around the mill.

27 Mr Leath and his waggon near Bridgnorth, 1912
Although the arrival of the nineteenth-century rail network improved the movement of goods and materials around the country the need for road transport from railway station to eventual destination remained. In the case of coal and other items required at Gatacre Hall this last link in the haulage chain was provided by Mr Leath, pictured here. He combined his duties as a carrier with the tenancy of an estate smallholding. The waggon in which his two children ride shows the design features of an east Shropshire vehicle at a period when substantial differences in shape and paint colour could still be observed from one part of the county to another. The projecting frame in front of the children is a harvest ladder, or extension, which enabled heavier loading of bulky loads.

29 Canal banksmen, Whixall, about 1900
Canals and railways too required regular maintenance. Railway tracks had to be kept up, bridges, embankments and signals inspected and made good, and on the canals locks and linings especially needed constant attention. More mundane tasks of an agricultural character were also required. Hundreds of miles of hedges and verges bounding tracks and tow paths had to be cut and mowed, and encroaching scrub removed.

Here a gang of banksmen on the Shropshire Union canal are cutting the grass along the canal bank near Whixall. The two men at the front with scythes are mowing, while at least one of those behind, Joseph George, is clearing the cut grass with a pitchfork or rake. The boat apparently forms part of the gang's equipment; perhaps the cut grass was collected in it. On the far side of the canal the grass seems already to have been mowed and the hedge cut.

Opposite:
28 A donkey cart, Horsehay, late nineteenth century
Very much a home-made product, photographed near Moreton Coppice Primitive Methodist chapel, Horsehay, on the industrial fringe of the Ironbridge Gorge. Many of the poorer inhabitants of the area combined the keeping of smallholdings with part-time industrial work, and such carts would have been most useful for carrying bags of coal or potatoes, as well as for practical, if hardly stylish, personal transport!

30 Ploughing near Shrewsbury, late nineteenth century
This photograph, taken during a pause in the cultivation of the heavy clay of Bank Farm, near Shrewsbury, shows two methods of harnessing horse teams. In the foreground a matched pair is working abreast to pull a single furrow, all-metal plough via the metal chains and wooden swingletrees seen behind the legs of the horses. Behind them are three horses harnessed in line with the one on the right (partly obscured) occupying the shafts — possibly of a roller or muck cart.

Once cultivated this ground was used to grow a fodder crop for the horses kept at Franklin's Livery Stables in Shrewsbury.

3 Cultivating and Sowing

The time-consuming task of preparing the ground for the sowing of crops marked the start of the arable farmer's year. Although the source of power for such cultivation evolved from oxen to horses and finally to the tractor, and the implements became refined over time, the processes remained largely unaltered. It was customary for the land first to be ploughed to bury the remains of the previous crop and to expose a fresh layer of soil. To help break down and consolidate the new surface harrows and rollers would be used, with the aim of providing a well-worked tilth to accommodate the seeds. These were originally broadcast by hand, which was slow and rather wasteful. Improvements in Victorian manufacturing technology enabled the prototype seed drills of the eighteenth century to become an affordable reality for all but the most marginal farmer by the middle of the twentieth century.

31 Ploughing at Stoke St Milborough, 1902

A commonplace scene on small family farms throughout the county, here captured by the photographer at New House Farm. Judging from the height of the corn and the dress of the workers it would appear to be a sunny summer's day. The ploughman is Henry Burton (died 1923), with his ten-year-old son Albert (died 1985) providing the encouragement for the cross-bred horse 'Tilley'. Although the harness shows signs of age and makeshift repairs, the plough (made by Howards of Bedford) appears relatively new.

Given a single-furrow plough, a strong horse and easy soil conditions the most that could be ploughed in a day was an acre. With the warm sun, the slope of the field and the already careworn look of Tilley half that amount would have been no mean achievement for the Burtons.

32   Ploughing at Llanfair Waterdine, 1905
In the hilly country on Shropshire's south-west border, good arable land is at a premium. Here ploughman Alfred Davies of the Goytre and his bearded father pose after cultivating an area of the valley bottom, with the grassy slopes of Lloyney Rock rising dramatically behind them. The harnessing of two horses side by side was a common pattern for ploughing, with one horse soon becoming accustomed to walking in the furrow.

33 Carting manure, Roden Lodge, Wem, about 1900
*A broad-wheeled manure cart about to leave the farmyard
behind three horses of the Shire type. Loading the vehicle with
the well-rotted straw and dung required both stamina and the
skilful wielding of a muck fork; unloading in the fields usually
involved the drawing-off of the muck into strategically-placed
piles, from where it was later spread by hand.*

Opposite:

34 Tractor-drawn manure spreader, late 1920s
*The arduous task of spreading manure on the fields by hand
remained common practice until the early twentieth century.
Mechanical relief from the drudgery of the muck fork came via
several designs of wheeled spreader, culminating in the type
illustrated here. This took the form of a flat-bedded waggon
which held the manure, a chain-driven device to move the
manure towards the back of the vehicle, and a revolving drum at
the rear to spread the muck. As all of the mechanical elements
of the implement were driven from the rear wheels, and the
weight of the loaded manure was considerable, it was always a
task best suited to tractor power.*

35 Sowing turnips near Clun, 1908
*The use of a drill to sow a crop had the great advantage of
distributing seed evenly in straight lines throughout a field. This
enabled the later use of a horse-drawn hoe, or scuffle, to control
the weeds emerging between the crop row and so increase
productivity.*

*The turnip drill in the photograph is being drawn by three
Shire horses. Similar drills survived in use as tractor-hauled
implements until the Second World War.*

36 Ridging ground for root crops near Newport, 1910
Once land intended for potato crops had been ploughed and worked to achieve a suitable tilth it would usually be re-ploughed to provide a pattern of ridges and intervening furrows. The implement used to make this corduroy-like texture is being drawn by the three horses in this photograph. Similar to the conventional plough in the design of its all-metal frame it was fitted with a pair of mouldboards that tapered to a point and formed ridges when drawn through the soil.

Following the ridge plough or 'ridger' across the field would be the planters — men, like those on the left of the photograph, who manually positioned the seed potatoes in the furrows. The final task in planting would be for the ridge plough to traverse the field again to split the previously-made ridges and thereby cover the seed. Using such a system would mean that the plants could grow along the ridges, enabling periodic earthing-up and easier weeding of the crop.

Note the housen worn on the collars of the two horses furthest from the camera. These semi-circular additions of leather, common in Scotland and the north of England, were designed to protect the vulnerable withers from the worst of the elements.

37 Mangold harvest near Oswestry, 1920s
Three youngsters pose behind a heap of mangold wurzels at Berghill Farm, Middleton. This root crop, being sensitive to frosts, required harvesting in the late autumn. It was usually stored in well-insulated clamps for feeding to livestock after Christmas. High in sugar content, mangolds were preferred to turnips as a dairy cow ration as they did not taint the milk. Large individual examples like those in the photograph were common on fertile soils, and given liberal use of manure, returns of 50 tons per acre could be achieved.

38 Stacking sugar beet near Chetwynd, 1930s

Between the wars the area of the county under the traditional root crop of mangolds, swedes and turnips declined as the folding of sheep and the winter feeding of cattle in yards became less profitable. Many farmers in the east of the county found sugar beet to be a viable alternative and the acreage under the new crop grew steadily. It was always most popular on farms close to processing plants like the one at Allscott, near Wellington, which was no doubt the destination of this harvest from Showell Grange, Sambrook.

39 Mowing team, Ludlow, about 1862

An early photograph showing the hay harvest underway in the valley of the River Teme, with Ludlow Castle rising prominently in the background. The four men of the mowing team all have their scythe blades in a similar position on the ground, and are presumably maintaining this posture to assist the photographer. The warm summer weather has reduced the workers to their shirt sleeves, clearly showing the sharpening stones hanging in pouches at the rear of their belts. As they progress from right to left in the photograph the team will take its pace from the leading man, with each member maintaining a safe distance from the man in front.

The grass in the foreground has been mown, and the men would appear to be approaching the fenced boundary of the field, which may explain the welcome sight of the jacketed farmer or landowner with flagon and mugs on the left.

4 Hay Harvest

Securing an adequate reserve of good quality hay was the principal summer task of all livestock farmers. With a well-stocked rickyard, and full hay loft, the winter months could be approached with a degree of assurance. For although root crops and concentrated corn rations also played their part in the winter diet of livestock, hay was the major sustainer of many farm animals in those months when the grass ceased to grow.

To ensure a good hay harvest in the fickle climate large numbers of the rural population would be enlisted. For many, including most women and children, it would be their major commitment in the farming calendar, and was looked upon as a social gathering as well as a seasonal task. Despite Victorian advances in engineering that provided machines that could cut, turn and collect hay, change came but slowly to the small mixed farms of the county. Only when the tractor-hauled baler moved onto the landscape in the years following the Second World War could the spell of the traditional ritual of haymaking by hand be said to have been broken.

40 Mechanised mowing on the Dudmaston estate, 1909
Although efficient grass cutting machines were in production before the time of the Ludlow scene (plate 39) their popularity was to come significantly later. Here, two well-matched horses are hitched to a mowing machine whose design altered only little during the best part of a century. Obscured by the crop lies the cutter bar resting upon wheels. Housed within the bar is a reciprocating blade comprising a series of triangular-shaped sections, and powered, via a system of gears, from one of the machine's land wheels.

When cut the grass would drop in broad bands or swathes which, once the upper surface had been dried, could be turned by hand or machine. By maintaining steady progress with such a mower it would have been possible in one hour to cut the acre that would have been a day's task for a skilled scytheman.

41 Haymaking near Craven Arms, about 1914

Once the grass was mown it would then require turning to ensure even drying. On smaller farms this continued to be done by hand well into this century. This clear photograph shows a family at work on the smallholding of John Boulton, in the centre of the scene, who combined small-scale farming with his job as the licensee of the Stokesay Castle Hotel in Craven Arms. He is assisted by his wife (to the left) and his sister (extreme right), who are using a wooden hay rake and a pitchfork or pikel respectively. At least two younger members of the family are preferring to rest in the drying crop in the background. Rather unusually none of the workers are wearing hats.

On the left of the picture can be seen the remains of last year's hay stack; judging from the bulky nature and texture of Mr Boulton's current crop it too would soon have been ready for carting to the rickyard.

42   Haymaking, south Shropshire

Should well-made, dry hay have to remain in the fields overnight it was prudent to pile it into cocks to minimise the damage caused by rain or a heavy dew. Several such cocks can be seen in this photograph. Once the outer surface of the cock had been restored to its previously crisp condition by sun and wind then the hay could be loaded.

There would appear to be a clear differentiation in tasks given to the workers in the photograph: four of the women can be seen holding hay rakes with which to collect the remaining hay, whilst the two men on the ground at the rear of the waggon would presumably have been responsible for pitching to their colleagues on the waggon. All of the adults wear headgear of varying styles (contrast with plate 41 opposite) with the bowler-hatted man on the right probably being the farmer. Note the newly-applied thatch roofs on the buildings behind the hayfield.

43 Hay harvest, Craven Arms, 1917
A second photograph showing haymaking on the smallholding belonging to the then landlord of the Stokesay Arms Hotel, Mr John Boulton, who is seated on the lower rungs of the ladder (see also plate 41). His wife is immediately behind him while several of the young ladies in the photograph could have been maids from the hotel called upon to help out at harvest-time. Although not all of the characters are likely to have worked to the same extent in collecting and loading the crop the photograph shows how the young and old of both sexes were drawn by this farm activity more than any other — a pattern reinforced by the wartime need for active men to fight for their country (see also plates 109 to 110).

The satisfactory nature of the harvest would appear to be reflected in the good humour of the workers, and is being toasted with the contents of the flagon in the hands of the elderly man second from the right. The load, although of rather modest proportions, would no doubt have been adjusted to suit the capabilities of the single horse whose ear coverings gave protection from irritating hay seeds and flies.

44   Haymaking near Onibury

Here the swathes of mown hay have been amalgamated by a horse-drawn machine into parallel 'windrows' across the field. That allowed a waggon to be drawn between the rows, enabling the hay to be loaded on from both sides. Judging from the lengthy shadows and the stage of the process it is likely to be early evening, with workers keen to secure as much of the crop as possible before nightfall. The laden waggon, which when empty could have weighed almost three-quarters of a ton, would certainly have required the effort of both horses to move it when loading was complete. Building a load was an art in itself, where mastery over the loose and yielding hay was only gained with experience.

45 Hay harvest, Ness Strange, about 1887
With the waggon safely loaded, an all-male labour force are enjoying their break or 'bait'. The horse in the shafts of the waggon appears to be a piebald, with a rather larger and darker animal in the traces. Standing in the foreground are two wooden-framed heel or stubble rakes. These were pulled along behind the operator to collect the last hay remaining in the field, and with a width of up to five feet and row of long, curved teeth they were equally efficient in corn or hay harvest.

46 Hay raking, Dudmaston estate, 1909

Even with the greatest care it was not possible for all of a hay crop to be gathered and loaded without a proportion remaining on the ground. The scattered remnants of the crop were initially collected with either a wooden hay rake (as shown in plate 41) or a larger heel rake (see plate 45), but as the nineteenth century progressed the more efficient horse-drawn hay rake became more widespread. This machine was pulled by a single horse and the hay was collected by a series of metal tines positioned slightly above ground level. When sufficient of the crop had been accumulated a lever could be operated to raise the tines and leave the rakings for collection later.

The photograph is one of a splendid series taken by Frances Pitt near Dudmaston, three miles south-east of Bridgnorth. As the horse continues at a steady pace across the field the operator is about to trip the rake to release the hay. In the background are cocks of hay ready for loading onto cart or waggon.

47 Rickyard scene, Dudmaston estate, 1909

The destination of the loaded waggons seen in the previous plates would have been the rickyard like the one shown in the photograph. On the right a horse is led back to the fields, its waggon empty save for three passengers. A second waggoner waits his turn to draw his horse alongside the new rick and begin the task of pitching the loose hay to the man on the top.

The new rick may well have been only half of its intended height when this photograph was taken. As it neared completion a pitched roof would have been built up with the last loads of hay. Over the ensuing weeks the hay would settle under its own accumulated weight, and only then could a thatch of straw be applied to keep the crop in good condition.

Beyond the new rick stands one from the previous year, reduced to a fraction of its original size by winter feeding to stock. The step in the face of the rick shows where the most recent section has been removed, and its tidy appearance bears testimony to the skill with which farm workers used the ungainly hay knife to slice through the compressed hay.

48 and 49   Mowing on the Dudmaston estate, 1907

Although the scythe had been in continuous use since Roman times for cutting grass for hay its use in the cereal harvest was less universal. The sickle and the bagging hook offered viable alternatives where labour remained abundant, and for those farmers seeking more rapid progress at harvest after 1850 then the reaping machine was an obvious choice. Indeed such was the popularity of the new harvesting machinery that by the end of Victoria's reign only one-fifth of Britain's corn crop was being cut by hand.

Before the mowing team began their work in earnest sharpening stones were used to provide a cutting edge on the long curved scythe blades. Such stones were often carried through the fields in pouches on the back of the mowers as can be seen in the second photograph. Each man would no doubt have favoured his own scythe, with its adjustable handles correctly positioned to suit his reach and swing. For cutting corn crops a lightweight wooden cradle was often fitted to the base of the shaft, to direct the cut corn to one side in a neat manner.

The progress of the mowers through the field would have appeared painfully slow by today's standards. One skilled man with a scythe could usually mow one acre of wheat, one and a half of barley or two acres of oats in a lengthy and tiring day. It would then be gathered, tied and stooked by a team of labourers that usually included a number of women and children.

5 Cereal Harvest

Traditionally the harvest of cereal crops — wheat, barley and oats — followed that of hay in the farming calendar. Although Shropshire was never a truly arable county, certain areas became renown for the cultivation of a type of corn. In the south-east the undulating land was largely tilled for wheat; in the central and northern dairying districts, barley was often preferred in the rotation; whilst oats were grown commonly in the upland regions of the south-west and north-west.

It was in the harvesting and processing of cereal crops that the greatest advances were made during the nineteenth century. In the early 1800s it was customary for crops to be reaped with a hook or scythe and tied by hand into sheaves. This labour-intensive system continued when the stored crop was threshed with a flail — valued winter work for farm labourers.

By the close of the century mechanisation had revolutionised harvesting tasks for all but the smallest farmer. Only a quarter of the harvest was still being cut by hand, and flail threshing was but a memory. In their wake came the reaper-binder and the threshing machine that were to characterise the cereal harvest until the 1950s.

50 Horse-drawn reaper/binder, Dudmaston estate, 1907

Although taken at the same time as the mowing scenes (plates 48 and 49), this photograph records an altogether different approach to the same task. The reaper-binder radically altered the corn harvest when it appeared on the scene in the final quarter of the nineteenth century. For whereas the mowing teams and the early horse-drawn harvesting machinery still required a following labour force to tie cut corn into sheaves, this new innovation was able to produce a bound sheaf automatically. Fewer workers were now needed in the harvest fields as stooking — the grouping of sheaves for drying on the stubble — was the only unmechanised task that remained. With sufficient and sustained horsepower the reaper-binder would cut about eight acres of corn in one day.

The three horses in the photograph are harnessed in a unicorn formation, with the young boy riding postillion on the leading horse. To the right of the man on the binder is a whip, close at hand should the horses need further encouragement.

51 Mealtime by the reaper/binder, Linley, 1942

An interlude in the wartime harvest in south-west Shropshire, as the Pryce family, together with a female visitor from Liverpool, rest next to their reaper/binder. The absence of any lines or reins resting on the machine, and the easy manner in which workers sit close to the binder, suggest that either the working horses had been unhitched, or that motive power was being supplied by a tractor.

The binder was an 'Albion', made in Leigh, Lancashire, by the firm of Harrison, McGregor and Co., and aptly illustrates the enduring virtues of good design: first introduced in 1894, there were surprisingly few modifications made by the manufacturer in the years up to the date of this photograph. Indeed the popularity of the reaper/binder was to further increase until a peak of over 150,000 machines was recorded in use in the harvest of 1950.

52   Oat harvest, Glazeley, about 1943

As a result of the government's drive for higher wartime food production, many areas of grassland were ploughed and planted to provide much needed corn crops. One such field at Manor farm, Glazeley, in the south-east of the county, is shown here. The tenant farmer, Mr Richard Page, in the dark suit, had undertaken to grow a crop of seed oats for Dalteys, and the firm's fieldsman is pictured inspecting the recently harvested crop. By any standards the crop looks a good one with a heavy head and a longer straw length than would be customary today. Grouped in orderly stooks each of four sheaves, the crop would have remained in the field to dry before being carted off for storage and subsequently threshing.

The farm buildings in the background of the photograph include a substantial brick barn with diamond-shaped latticework to supply ventiliation for a stored crop.

53   Bringing in the harvest, near Broseley, early 1900s

Once the sheaves of corn had dried in the summer's sun and breeze, they were carted to a convenient location to await threshing. Depending upon the urgency of obtaining seed for sowing or sale and the availability of threshing equipment this wait could be a matter of weeks or one of several months.

Here a loaded vehicle is being drawn by a pair of powerful, though unmatched, horses on Linley farm, near Broseley, in a scene no doubt typical of harvest fields throughout the country. The young man at the head of the leading horse is proudly holding a long-handled pitchfork or pickel that in trained hands made the building of a high load an easier task.

54   Carrying beans near Shrewsbury, 1919

Field beans are a leguminous crop able to be grown on some of the heaviest clay land, and consequently well suited to midland soils. They can be sown either in autumn or spring, depending upon the variety, and when well-manured can provide a heavy crop of stock food.

Harvesting the crop usually involved a horse-drawn reaper-binder. Once the stooked crop had dried in the fields it was moved into storage to await threshing, and it is likely that this is the task recorded by the photographer at Harlescott House farm. Once threshed the beans were commonly ground and blended with cereals to produce a balanced livestock ration much favoured by dairy farmers.

55 and 56 Threshing near Bishop's Castle, 1901

When the Alderson family moved to farm at Lower Lea, near Bishop's Castle in 1901 they had various scenes from their first year of occupation recorded by a photographer. Two of the surviving prints show threshing underway alongside the timber-clad barn in the centre of the hamlet of Lea.

The principal character in this rural drama was the contractor who usually provided the steam engine and threshing machine. In the first photograph he can be seen standing to the left of his engine. The machine is of the portable type, off which power could only be taken via its large flywheel. Unable to move under its own steam, the engine and its accompanying threshing machine would have been hauled from farm to farm by horses as one by one the farmers played host to the contractor.

The newly-arrived farmer, William Alderson (1864–1918), stands alongside the engine with a pail of water while his two sons, Maurice and Tom, rest on the waggon. This vehicle is of the Montgomeryshire pattern and has a harvest ladder or extension protruding over the shafts to enable heavier loading of bulky produce. In this case the vehicle is being loaded with sacks of corn removed from the threshing box immediately behind it.

The full extent of the thresher is revealed in the second photograph. The harvested sheaves of corn would appear to have been stored in the large barn and were probably being pitched through the dooway behind the figures on top of the thresher. It would be their job to 'feed' the machine — a task that had its dangers and its casualities from the unguarded rotating drum. The threshed and cleaned corn would emerge from the end of the machine closest to the steam engine, whilst the straw would be expelled from the opposite end. This was being pitched onto a vehicle before being stored in readiness for later use as bedding or for feeding to stock.

57   Threshing at Neen Savage, 1908

Although the first effective threshing machine had been built as early as 1786, technical improvements to the threshing process were still being made over a century later. This scene at Overwood Farm, Neen Savage, records the initial steaming of a new traction engine, which was supplying power, via the sagging belt, to the thresher. This type of steam engine was able to move under its own power and represented a considerable investment on the part of the owner. To ensure an effective and uneventful beginning to its working life the manufacturers of the engine — Fosters of Lincoln — sent one of their own mechanics to accompany it for ten days. In the photograph he can be seen with his hand upon the engine's large driving wheel, whilst the new owner, William Griffiths, stands proudly on the engine with his son Jack.

Elsewhere in the photograph are clues that this is an efficient and modern farm. The four-bay Dutch Barn in the background is a substantial structure, making good use of the recently popularised corrugated iron sheet as a cladding material. Immediately behind the threshing machine lurks a straw trusser, with one of its pair of tall all-metal wheels just visible. Introduced from the 1880s, these machines retied the threshed straw into convenient bundles for easier handling. With ease and comfort again in mind the sack lifting truck being operated in front of the thresher used a simple ratchet mechanism to help the worker raise the filled sack to a height from where he could more readily lift it onto his back.

58 Threshing near Llanfair Waterdine, about 1920

This photograph from the south-western extremes of the county vividly illustrates the co-operative spirit that underlay the labour-intensive efforts of threshing. In this rolling field at Wernygeufron farm fourteen people from three families are busily engaged in serving the threshing machine, which, as Thomas Hardy observed, could keep up a 'despotic demand upon the endurance of their muscles and nerves'.

At the time of the photograph, Wernygeufron was about to welcome new tenants onto its land — the Merediths, who, judging from the nameboard on the cart, had moved from Beguildy in neighbouring Radnorshire. They were assisting the outgoing tenants — the Turleys — with the threshing of their corn. In a practical and equable division of the fruits of their labours, the Turleys took the grain with them whilst the Merediths retained the bulky straw on their new holding.

Providing the power for the two threshing families is the aged portable engine of Mr Breeze who stands at the rear of his machine. This machine is distinguished by an unusual homemade sectional chimney; like all engines it consumed significant quantities of water during a day's work, and was no doubt replenished from the large barrel on a regular basis.

The threshed corn is being loaded onto the Turley's waggon which shows many of the features of a locally-made vehicle. A horse's bridle lies on the shafts of the waggon waiting until a lull in the noisy threshing activity enables animal power to re-emerge onto the scene.

59 Baling straw, Cound, 1916

Although stationary balers were in use prior to the First World War, the conflict encouraged their more widespread adoption. As more and more horses were requisitioned by the army, so its demand for hay and straw grew. For efficient transportation these bulky crops had to be baled on the farms, and numbers of stationary balers like the Ruston example in the picture were purchased by the War Department. Powered from the traction engine and manned by a mixture of army and civilian personnel, it successfully compressed and tied the bales thirty years before the age of the mobile pick-up baler.

60   Threshing contractors, 1920s

Due to the high capital costs involved in mechanised threshing it was usually the province of the itinerant contractor. The advent of the self-propelled traction engine eased the problems of movement from farm to farm and also enabled a threshing machine to be towed at the same time. The machine on the extreme right is a straw trusser which tied the loose, threshed straw into more manageable bundles. This particular example was made by the firm of Howards of Bedford.

  In the background of the photograph are two contrasting styles of crop storage, the Dutch Barn and the traditional straw rick. The man standing on the rick looks to be preparing it for a weatherproof thatch.

61   Whimberry pickers, Bucknell, about 1900

Whimberries, the local name for bilberries or whortleberries, that is the fruit of the dwarf hardy shrub Vaccinium myrtillus, *formerly grew in profusion across the county's uplands. Although edible, the chief importance of the blue-black berries in the later nineteenth and early twentieth century was as a dye base, used in the northern textile manufactories.*

Around the Stiperstones and the Long Mynd, for instance, the school holidays began when the whimberries were ripe and continued until there were no more to pick. In some years blackberries might then be picked as well, and the holidays further extended. At this time whimberry buyers in the Clun area alone were paying out £500 a year, sometimes as much as £800, and for smallholders and other rural poor the additional income was a welcome supplement to the family budget. That berry picking was almost exclusively an activity for women and children is clearly shown in this photograph, taken outside the Old School House, a general store and bakery.

74

6   Fruit and Horticulture

Shropshire has never been a county noted for fruit growing or for market gardening. Admittedly most farmhouses had an orchard, and many cottages an apple tree or two, but that was mainly for home consumption, whether as fruit or as cider. Similarly fruit, nuts, and berries growing wild in hedgerows and woods were all collected, but again normally for use in the home. One or two exceptions can be pointed out, mostly fairly insignificant, where the activity was on at least a semi-commercial scale, an opportunity more often than not created by the improved road and rail links of the later nineteenth century: of these the annual whimberry picking season is perhaps the best example.

Only in the Teme valley, in the extreme south-east of the county between Ludlow and Cleobury Mortimer, was there any concentration on fruit growing, especially apples. Here, where the Clee Hills slope southward, is the northern limit of the Worcestershire and Herefordshire fruit growing region. Cider apple trees were most numerous, but cherries and damsons were also grown.

In Shropshire as a whole the peak acreage of 4,846 for orchards was reached in 1900. By 1937 it had fallen to under 3,000, although in the Teme valley the decline came later, and in the 1930s between ten and twenty *per cent* of the farmland there was still occupied by orchards.

62   **Whimberry pickers, the Long Mynd, 1899**
A charming picture, but one which gives no impression of what hard work berry picking was.

63 Cider making, Bucknell area, about 1900

In the later nineteenth century the ancient art of cider making saw something of a revival, and in 1900 there were almost 5,000 acres of orchards in Shropshire. That acreage was principally in the south and east of the county, really an extension of the Worcestershire and Herefordshire fruit growing region.

The employment here of a steam engine and nine men suggests production on a semi-commercial scale. The engineer (on extreme left) drives a hopper-topped mill or 'scratter' which mashed the apples. The pulp was then made into 'cheeses', sandwiched between hair cloths in the big screw presses. As these were tightened the juice ran out into the broad, shallow vat, from which it was bucketed into the large barrels ready on the cart for carriage to the store. In this case that store was apparently in Herefordshire, as indicated by the plate on the cart. During the storage period the raw cider would ferment, impurities escaping with the froth through a hole in the top of the hogshead. Once fermentation was complete the barrel would be corked and left to mature, usually for at least six months.

Opposite:

64 Pressing apples, Buckridge Bank Farm, early 1940s
Cider making on an altogether different scale, on the Shropshire-Worcestershire county border. Charles and Iris Worrall are using a press made about 1930 by Bill Ankrett, a Kidderminster carpenter.

65   The glasshouses, Roden, 1930s
Since the eighteenth century the great landed estates had had glasshouses to grow their own produce, and in the nineteenth century there were various commercial operations using them to grow vegetables for consumption in the surrounding towns. The Co-operative Wholesale Society opened a small factory for jam and bottled fruit at Roden before the First World War, and practically the whole village became involved. Some of the fruit was grown outdoors, but there were also large areas under glass. Here straw is being dug in to assist drainage.

66 Watercress beds at Hinstock, early twentieth century

Watercress, Nasturtium officinale, *can be found growing wild along the banks of many British streams. Since the early nineteenth century various parts of the country have seen its cultivation in artificial, plank-lined beds along streams or man-made channels. Water in the beds is maintained at a depth of about ten centimetres, and using this system about a dozen crops can be produced each year.*

Watercress growing is not normally associated with Shropshire, but in the early twentieth century there were three separate systems of beds in Hinstock parish, in the north-east of the county. The largest system was that beside the mill pond at Shakeford, which supplied large quantities of watercress to the Potteries district of Staffordshire. A second set of beds was at Bearcroft Pool, run as a sideline by the local butcher. Pictured here are the beds off Pixley Lane, which went out of use soon after the First World War. Although the industry is remembered to have thrived it was laborious and uncomfortable work, and tended to produce rheumatic complaints.

67 Cleaning the fishpond, Dudmaston, 1934

From the early Middle Ages most substantial households had one or more fishponds where fish were bred and fattened ready for the table. Species such as bream, roach, tench, pike, and from the fifteenth century carp, were all carefully managed in this way. Records show that traditional farmhouse fishponds remained in use until the later nineteenth century, and T. H. Williams of Shrewsbury was still advertising himself as a coracle and net maker, available by contract to fish pools and lakes, as late as 1899. Those pools which survived into the twentieth century tended to be principally ornamental in function, as at Dudmaston.

The ponds, just as much as their stock, required regular maintenance. Some were formed by dams being thrown across streams, whereas others were entirely artificial excavations, usually rectangular, fed by a spring or via a leat. Whichever, all had wooden sluices and fixtures that needed periodic attention, and all needed to be drained once every few years to have the accumulated silt and weeds cleaned out. As the picture suggests, the work was laborious, dirty, and slow.

7 Livestock

Traditionally most farms kept a wider range of livestock than is found on today's more specialised holdings. An element of self-sufficiency remained on most farms until comparatively recently, with supplies of dairy produce, eggs and home-killed bacon being produced for the household. A degree of interdependence between different crops and animals was also established, with pigs being reared on dairy by-products, sheep folded to manure arable ground, and poultry being fed on home-grown corn.

Interest in improving the quality and productivity of livestock began in the eighteenth century as pioneers such as Bakewell undertook selective breeding experiments. Further work continued into the nineteenth century as types of animal became standardised into breeds and then achieved widespread acceptance. The popularity of a particular breed was often enhanced by the work of a specialist breed society, which would promote sales and record pedigrees of stock. Three locally important breeds had their fortunes improved by such efforts: the Hereford breed of cattle, which in 1846 had the first volume of its Herd Book published; the Shire Horse, whose evolution from the War Horse was completed by the formation of a Breed Society in 1878; and the Shropshire Sheep, which in 1882 became the world's first breed to have a flock book society.

68   Off to Bishop's Castle Show, about 1910
The Aldersons who farmed at Lower Lea, near Bishop's Castle (see also plates 55 to 56) were noted horse breeders. Here a selection of healthy and well-presented horses is being taken to the local agricultural show by members of the family. William Alderson, the tenant farmer at Lea, was a founder of the local Shire Horse Society. He met a premature death in 1918 after being hit by a waggon drawn by a runaway horse team.

69   The travelling stallion

As the nineteenth century progressed more attention was given to improving the breeding and character of the working farm horse. Several societies were established in the 1870s to cater for the distinct breeds of British working horse and the Shire grew to be the popular choice of Shropshire's farmers. For the average man the keeping of a stallion would have been impractical and expensive. Instead, enterprising breeders or local associations would bring well-bred animals to stand at stud for a season. Their availability would be advertised in the locality, and it is presumably to this end that the fine animal in the photograph was being paraded at a local show in the Bishop's Castle area. He is thought to be 'Bramhope Gay Duke' — a stallion used by the local Alderson family — and was brought to the area from Cheshire. He looks to be a sound example, with the sought-after four white legs, and is no doubt attracting comment from the group of men on the right.

70   Mare in farmyard, Tugford, 1905

Little is known about the subjects of this photograph, although it contains several interesting details. The Piebald mare may lack the conformation and presentation of the horses in the previous two photographs, but it was probably more typical of the working horse found on many Shropshire farms in the early twentieth century. Her mane and tail are long and unkempt, while the matted 'feathers' or longer hair on her legs may point to some Shire ancestry.

Behind the horse is the remains of a hay rick, or stack. Built of lose, unbaled hay in a previous summer, it looks to be much reduced in size, to the point where two timber props may be supporting what remains. The clean face of the rick is the result of the required hay being cut out with a large-bladed hay knife. This also accounts for the ladder that leans against the far side of the rick, as the worker would begin a vertical cut at the height of the thatched roof and progress downwards with a sawing action.

71 and 72 Timber hauling

Some of the largest horse teams were to be seen when timber was being hauled to the sawmill. The vehicle usually chosen for the task would be a timber carriage — a substantial, four-wheeled machine whose wheelbase could be adjusted to suit the length of the load being carried.

In the first photograph a line of seven horses pauses whilst fording the River Severn at Hampton Loade. The river would appear to be at its summer level, enabling an easier crossing. Several other lengths of round timber lie at the top of the ramp leading down to the moored passenger ferry.

The second photograph shows timber being removed from Spoonhill wood, near Much Wenlock, in July 1915. To provide sufficient power, two teams of Shires have been hitched to the load, with the cart saddle worn by the fifth in line betraying his normal position within a vehicle's shafts.

See also plates 119 to 121 on the timber industry.

73 Horse team at Onibury

A scene from the inter-war years as a waggoner remembered only as 'Master Jack' drives his team of three down the lanes of south Shropshire. The vehicle is a robust dray, well-suited to carrying a variety of heavy loads. The horses are harnessed in an unusual formation, with the rear 'shaft' horse being preceded by a pair of trace horses, each linked by chains to one of the shaft blades. With this arrangement, known as a 'pick-axe' formation, the waggoner had direct control over all three horses by holding either bridle or reins. He nevertheless retains a whip under his arm, no doubt for encouraging the lead pair.

74 Three Shropshire yearling rams, Culmington, 1920s

The Shropshire breed of sheep had its origins in the indigenous stock of the county's upland regions. Careful breeding during the second half of the nineteenth century improved the leggy, slow-maturing and lightly-fleeced native sheep to the level of those in the photograph — well-fleshed and heavily woolled. Indeed, the amount of wool on the heads of these rams could well be considered excessive by modern standards. It was one of several traits bred into the Shropshire to satisfy the demands of overseas purchasers who provided a lucrative market for home breeders in the early decades of the twentieth century.

The breeder of these rams was Mr Lockhart of Culmington, whose sheep are accompanied in the photograph by Mr Edwards, the shepherd at Culmington, and by Mr Edwards' son. The leg crook held by Mr Edwards was the time-honoured way of catching individual members of a flock; the small terrier, although not a typical sheepdog, may also have assisted.

75 Sheep washing, Tugford, 1905

Before sheep were shorn it was customary for them to be washed to remove insects and other impurities from the wool. This could be accomplished by simply driving them across a river, although better results would be obtained by damming a watercourse to produce a greater depth.

In this Edwardian scene at Tugford, in the south of the county, the collected sheep would appear to be penned between the two sheep cratches on the right. When driven down to the bank they would be encouraged to jump into the water by the bowler-hatted man. His two colleagues, balancing on a ladder that spans the water, are ensuring that each animal is fully immersed and cleaned before being allowed to swim to the opposite bank.

Once washed the sheep would be left for about a week before shearing, so as to give the wool time to dry and regain its natural oils.

76   Sheep shearing, Craven Arms, 1932

Sheep were traditionally shorn when the onset of warmer weather encouraged the fleece to 'rise' with natural oils. Such a secretion would make the fleece heavier, an important consideration when wool is sold by weight, as well as easing the shearer's task.

Until the beginning of the nineteenth century the most common shearing tools were shaped like large pairs of scissors and were usually the product of the local blacksmith. They were gradually superseded by sprung shears with two triangular blades connected by a loop of spring steel — a popular design of which many examples still survive. Only at the onset of the twentieth century did the technique of hand clipping give way to the earliest type of mechanised shearing, as seen in the photograph. This used the rotary action of the hand-turned wheel to power, via a flexible drive, a shearing head in which the reciprocating teeth cut the wool. This invention changed the technique of shearing and paved the way for electrically-powered machines with broadly-similar shearing heads.

Shearing has long been a branch of farming where workers could pit their skills against each other, and this scene shows Messrs G. Preece (left) and J. Edwards shearing their way to the Silver Cup in the Young Farmers' county competition of 1932. In such a contest the contribution of the wheel turner — like Jim Williams in cap and striped shirt — was vital.

77 Sheep dipping, south Shropshire

The flocks of the nineteenth-century farmer were susceptible to a variety of ills, including foot rot, liver fluke, lung worms and sheep scab. This last ailment was initially treated by the application of a salve to the skin of the sheep to kill the causative mite and thereby prevent subsequent itching and loss of condition. As the nineteenth century progressed it became more customary for sheep to be immersed in a chemical solution. The success of this method eventually gave rise to legislation to ensure the compulsory dipping of sheep by the close of the century.

In this early twentieth-century farmyard scene the sheep are being dipped in a simple wooden trough. Each animal would be inverted in the liquid by the two operators, who no doubt got soaked with quantities of dip from time to time. Once all of the animal had been covered by the solution it was lifted clear of the trough and rested upon the sloping draining board. When most of the dip had drained from the fleece the animal was slid down the ramp on the right and allowed to rejoin the flock.

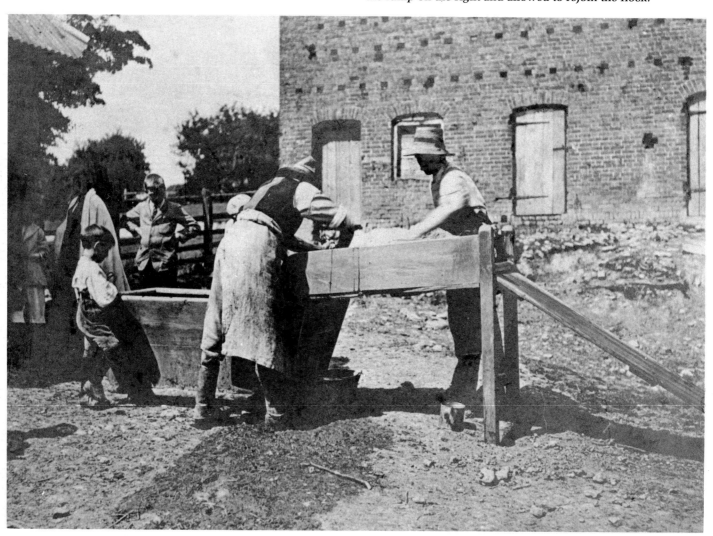

78 Sheep dipping near Oswestry, 1930s

The advantages of the simple dipping apparatus in plate 77 were its low cost and mobility. On farms with large flocks of sheep the investment in a permanent trough and collecting yard became customary during the inter-war years.

In this summer scene at Whitehall Farm, Aston, the confined sheep are waiting to enter the dipping bath. Once immersed their progress through the dip would be controlled by the man in the foreground, who would ensure that each animal was thoroughly soaked. Note the contrast between the freshly-shorn, long-tailed ewes and the well-grown, woolly lambs.

79   Bull at Glebe Farm, Diddlebury, about 1908

At the time of the photograph Glebe Farm was owned by Edwin Cox, a farmer best known as a breeder of Hackney horses. The quality of his stock bull, a Hereford, shows that he was no mean breeder of cattle too. Little is known of the bull's sidesaddle rider who was known simply as Jackson, but from his familiarity with the animal one may presume him to be one of Farmer Cox's farmworkers.

The building in the background looks to have been recently re-roofed with corrugated iron sheets — a building material that infiltrated many an agricultural scene from the late nineteenth century onwards.

80   Hereford bull in sale ring

An attentive audience of farmers and dealers casts expert eyes over Lot 62 at this late nineteenth-century farm sale. The auctioneers, Jackson and McCartney, were famous for their sales at Craven Arms and Ludlow, and it is likely that this sale also took place in the South Shropshire countryside. The impressive Hereford bull is being restrained by means of a bull staff, clipped to a ring in its nose.

Hereford cattle had earned a justifiable world-wide reputation as hardy beef animals by this date. Although nowadays recognised by their distinct 'red with white face' colouring, this was only one of several alternatives found in the emerging breed of the early nineteenth century. Note the impressive horns, well-nigh universal in cattle of the period.

81 Death by lightning, Upton Cressett, 1945

A sad reminder of the ease with which stock can be lost by disease or accident. Ten bloated corpses lie beneath the hedgerow where the cattle had sought shelter from a storm, leaving Upton Cressett farmer Mr J. Price to count the cost.

Insurance against such mishaps was provided by a number of companies specialising in agricultural risks. Notable amongst these is the National Farmers Union Mutual Insurance Society, which was established in 1910 to encourage farmers to join a newly-formed farmers' union.

82 Cow at Villa Farm, Hinstock

Here one is struck by the almost bashful look of handler and cow as they pose for the camera at the Hinstock farm of Mrs Morgan. Her cow looks to be a Shorthorn, albeit a rather undistinguished example of the breed that was pre-eminent in Britain's dairies during the first half of the twentieth century. It is held by William Wild, a brother of Mrs Morgan, whose small stature serves to flatter the build of the cow.

83 Pigs at Ticklerton, 1890

By the late eighteenth century Shropshire was fast gaining a reputation for its pig rearing, and there developed a habit of calling most well-bred, largely-white pigs 'Shropshires'. While the practice had died out a century later the importance of pigs to the farming economy continued, and in 1882 it was estimated that there was one pig for every four of the county's residents.

The nineteenth-century pig usually enjoyed more freedom than do his twentieth-century descendents. Here two well-grown examples named 'Tommie' and 'Bessie' rest in the straw in a Ticklerton farmyard. They both appear to have the coarse wiry coat, prick ears and long snout of the Tamworth breed — a hardy type, well-suited to an outdoor life.

84   Farmyard near Bishop's Castle, about 1900

In this picture of the Alderson's family farm, the yard is populated with a commonplace mixture of poultry and a well-grown pig. The cross-bred pig, along with many others, probably met its end on the farm in the building on the right of the photograph. The killing and butchering were forbidden sights for the younger members of a family, although the noise associated with the 'sticking' would have been audible to all.

85 Chickens near Worthen, about 1908

Domestic fowl are generally accepted to have evolved from jungle fowl of the Far East. The early development of poultry in this country had more to do with the sport of cock fighting than a need for food, and those birds that were kept on farms were usually given only the most basic care and attention. This situation changed quite markedly in the mid nineteenth century as new breeds arrived on our shores from Asia and Europe. Foremost among these new birds was the Cochin, which varied considerably from previously-known types in its golden colour, large size, and in the fact that it laid brown, rather than white eggs. This surge of interest in poultry-keeping was encouraged by Queen Victoria, who kept her own flock at Windsor. As the number of breeds grew so did the classes at the fledgling poultry shows held around the country.

By the end of the nineteenth century the imported breeds had given poultry breeders the raw materials for the development of major British poultry types. Various breeds were standardised and some are probably present in the photograph of Mrs Ewell feeding her birds at Brockton Mill. It was quite common for millers to maintain flocks of poultry and to feed them with any surplus or sub-standard grain that came their way. Less customary would have been Mrs Ewell's costume as routine wear in a farmyard, and it is probable that the outfit was chosen with the photographer in mind.

86 Feeding the chickens, Bishop's Castle, 1902

Although many poultry fanciers aimed to show their stock they were always outnumbered by small-scale breeders who kept birds for more practical purposes. A few hens, together with a backyard pig, graced many a garden in both town and country, and both provided an important part of the family's diet. The multi-coloured chickens shown in the photograph are likely to have been hatched by a broody hen sitting on a range of bought-in eggs from a selection of different breeds. Behind the tail of the single mature hen is a broody coop, within which a hen could be restrained to quietly sit on eggs for the required 21 days. When in position the three slats on the front left of the coop would enable newly-hatched chicks to venture outside, but would restrain the hen for as long as was required to ensure a satisfactory hatch.

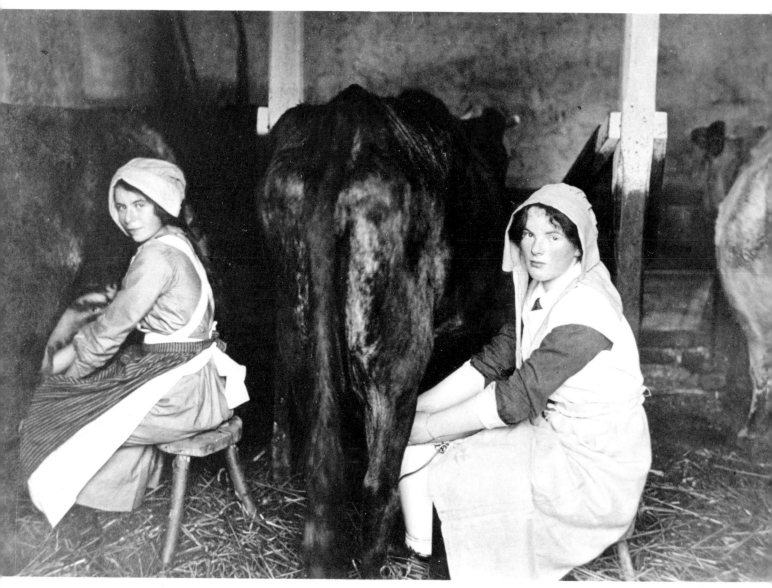

87 Learning dairying, north Herefordshire, about 1915
In the later nineteenth century interest began to stir at both national and county government levels in agricultural education. In 1888, for instance, a privately organized Agricultural and Dairy Conference at Ludlow formed part of a national campaign to encourage better butter and cheese making. Occasional demonstrations on the same topics began to be staged, as at Willey for Lord Forester's tenants in 1889.

In Shrewsbury, the Shropshire Technical School for girls, opened at Radbrook in 1901, became an important centre for teaching good dairying practice. Many of its pupils were farmers' daughters, who on completion of the course returned to manage their home dairies. Mary Edwards (on right), a Herefordshire girl who later moved to Shropshire where her family still farm, was a student on similar courses in Herefordshire. In 1913 and 1914 she attended ten-day courses at travelling day schools, and in 1915 a four-week poultry and dairying school run by the county council's Agriculture Department. Here, with a well dressed fellow student, she is learning to milk a shorthorn and holds the bucket in the correct position with her knees.

8 Dairying and Cheesemaking

In the later sixteenth and seventeenth centuries north Shropshire, with Cheshire, emerged as a specialist dairying farming region. By 1720 'great quantities' of Cheshire cheese were being made, and inventories reveal just how important dairying was to north Shropshire's farmers. Farmhouses by then usually included among their rooms both dairies for the processing of milk products and cheese storage chambers: many farmers died with several tons of cheese shelved therein, worth as much as several dozen cows. At this time the predominant type was probably the Longhorn, the milk from the cattle of Cheshire and the other northern counties being excellent for making cheese. In the earlier nineteenth century Longhorns were superseded by improved Shorthorns, themselves replaced in the mid twentieth century by Friesians.

By the mid twentieth century improved distribution facilities for liquid milk had precipitated a decline in farmhouse cheesemaking. This change was accelerated by the establishment of the Milk Marketing Board in 1933. Nevertheless, some farmhouse cheese was still made in north Shropshire in the 1990s.

Until the advent of mechanical milking parlours in the 1930s milking and dairying was very much the preserve of the farmer's wife and the female farm servants. What was required was not brute strength but dexterity, care and cleanliness, while the proximity of the dairy to the farmhouse allowed a woman to combine work there with her everyday chores such as minding children, providing meals, and dealing with tradesmen.

88 A dairymaid, Baschurch, 1920
When Jenny Gwilt ('Ginty') was a dairymaid at Slater's Farm, Baschurch, all milking in the county was still done by hand. Although the first milking machine was invented in 1862, and British, European, and American manufacturers had models on the market by the 1890s, the idea of mechanised milking did not catch on until the Second World War.

Much of the milk produced in Shropshire in the 1920s went to supply the Birmingham market. Liquid milk production and sales increased considerably in the 1930s as milk processing factories opened or, as at Minsterley, expanded, and especially after the formation in September 1933 of the Milk Marketing Board. This, for the first time, guaranteed producers a fixed price for their milk, and thus a more secure income. As a consequence farmers were more willing to invest in improvements, such as new milking parlours. By the end of the Second World War fifty per cent of the national herd was milked by machine, and accredited herds were becoming less of a novelty.

89   Delivering milk, Clun area, early 1920s
Only after the First World War did the bottling of milk become common. Until then milk sellers like Sarah Dyke, pictured here, made door-to-door deliveries dispensing milk as required from a churn. Pint and half-pint measures were used to ladle out the milk, which would then be poured into the waiting housewife's jug. Sarah Dyke's round was apparently sufficiently profitable for her later to trade in her hand cart for a pony and trap.

90   Delivering milk, Bishop's Castle, about 1930
Doris and Eddie Evans of New House Farm, Bishop's Castle, had a milk round in the 1920s and 1930s delivering milk produced on their father's farm to customers in Bishop's Castle — one of several such enterprises around the town at the time.

91   Churning butter, Aston, near Oswestry, 1930s

Requiring less space and equipment than cheese making, butter making was widely practised on farms and smallholdings. Before churning began the cream had to be separated, originally by allowing the milk to stand in a settling dish but from the 1890s using a mechanical separator.

Various mechanical aids were available to make butter, such as the plunger churn, the rocker churn, and the box churn. From the late eighteenth century, however, the various types of barrel churn gradually gained favour. Earliest were horizontal ones; end-over-end barrel churns, such as is seen here, became popular in the later nineteenth century.

The churn would first be washed out with salt water to prevent the cream and butter sticking. The cream would then be poured in at one end (seen upwards in this photograph, the top secured by wing nuts), and the churn turned until the butter 'came'. In the winter a little warm water might be added to quicken the process. Here, on Whitehill Farm, Aston, Beatrice Edwards' daily task of butter making has been much eased by the installation of a small engine, off which a pulley belt has been taken to turn the churn.

Once churned the butter was finished off by the excess water being removed in a 'butterworker' trough. It could then be patted into blocks or rolls ready for sale.

92 To market with butter, about 1900
Unfortunately nothing is known about this elderly lady, who is apparently about to set off to market with a consignment of butter. The baskets, known as 'butter flats' and probably of local manufacture, were specially designed to carry butter.

Not all the butter produced in Shropshire was of an acceptable quality. By the later nineteenth century roots were used as winter cattle food on all but the smallest of farms, and in 1895 much of the butter made in the county was said to have 'an objectionable turnip flavour'!

93 Leaving for Whitchurch cheese fair, 1920s
Some of north Shropshire's farmhouse cheese producers sold their cheese directly off the farm to dealers. Perhaps far more, however, was sold by the farmers themselves at the great cheese fairs held every three weeks at Ellesmere, Market Drayton, Shrewsbury, Wem and Whitchurch.

In the 1920s, when this photograph was taken of William Hockenhull setting off from Steel Grange, Prees Heath, for Whitchurch's fair with a load of Cheshire cheese, Shropshire was one of England's four largest cheese producing counties. Whitchurch, the biggest of the county's fairs, saw an average of 1,411 tons of cheese sold each year in the 1920s.

94　Cattle in High Street, Bishop's Castle

In many small Shropshire market towns sales of livestock were originally conducted in the streets, where to the bustle of a busy market day would be added the noisy and somewhat hazardous presence of the freely-roaming animals.

In Bishop's Castle a purpose-built livestock market replaced the more informal street sales in about 1914. The buildings shown in the photograph remain largely unaltered, however, with the Town Hall clock tower (centre) still dominating the intriguing architectural mix in the main street.

9 Markets and Fairs

During the nineteenth and early twentieth centuries, the market town was the hub around which rural activity revolved. It provided an opportunity for the inhabitants of the surrounding countryside to both buy and sell through an established weekly market or at one of the periodic fairs. Such gatherings of farmers and others from the then-isolated rural communities could give them a chance to meet for business or pleasure, to visit the bank or to take a market-day lunch with friends.

Most of the county's towns boasted a general market at this time, where farm produce such as eggs, butter and cheese would be sold. Indeed the dairying districts of North Shropshire produced such substantial quantities of cheese that these were sold in special markets, notably at Whitchurch. The livestock being sold at market would originally have been walked from the farm to the town, where farmer and dealer would strike a deal between themselves. Organised auction sales of stock were often only introduced when buying and selling moved from the town's streets to purpose-built premises. Usually housed in a separate building would be sales of corn, although Shropshire's limited output of cereal crops meant that it did not need the impressive Corn Exchanges of corn-growing counties of the south and east. Instead, sales were often conducted on the street and in public houses, or quantities of grain were moved directly from the farm to the local mill.

Along with the regular commitment of a weekly market, most towns developed a number of fairs on specified days throughout the year. These were often for selling a particular commodity, depending upon the season — breeding stock in spring, wool in early summer, and fatstock in the autumn. In addition to these was usually a May Fair at which farm servants traditionally sought new employment and then enjoyed the visiting entertainments and sideshows.

95 Walking to market, Church Stretton, about 1900
For the inhabitants of Shropshire's remoter districts, getting to the nearest market town could mean a journey of several miles. For many farmers this involved a ride in market cart or trap, while the poorer market-goers relied for the most part on walking. The lady in the foreground of this photograph combined her energies with that of the horse to transport produce from her smallholding on the western flanks of the Long Mynd to Church Stretton on the eastern side. As she nears the end of her journey she passes a group of ladies sporting the fashions of the day, which contrast with her rougher, more practical outfit.

96 Market Hall, Church Stretton, about 1900

The destination of the smallholder with her horse in plate 95 would have been Church Stretton's Market Hall, which fronted onto the High Street in the centre of this small town. This stone and brick building was erected in 1839 at a cost of £1,000, and replaced an earlier timber-framed structure. Each Thursday it was the scene of brisk trading as produce from surrounding farms was sold inside its ground floor arches and manufactured goods like the baskets in the foreground were traded from the 'pitches' outside. Beyond the Hall is the Plough public house and facing it is the Lion — both well-positioned to quench the thirsts of market-goers.

The Market Hall survived until 1963, when it was demolished after being declared unsafe. The Thursday market persists, however, on its former site.

97 Sheep and horse fair, Church Stretton, about 1905

By the close of the nineteenth century six fairs were held each year in Church Stretton. They included the popular hiring and mop fair in May, when farm servants traditionally changed employers, and the July wool fair. On September 25th came another great gathering as sheep, colts and horses were traded on the conveniently situated triangular plot at the foot of the Burway — the road that climbed out of the town towards the Long Mynd. Wooden pens erected against the perimeter walls and alongside the lower road provided secure housing for the substantial numbers of sheep that were driven to the fair. Many farmers appear to have ridden into town, leaving their horses saddled up while they conduct their business. The horses and ponies wearing only halters are likely to have been the ones for sale.

98   Cattle sale, Craven Arms area, early 1900s
*As this photograph testifies, not all livestock sales were
conducted through established markets, and it was generally
more convenient for dispersal sales of stock and machinery and
annual draft sales of surplus livestock to take place on the farm
concerned. Although the location and occasion of this sale are
not recorded it is probably a regular sale of cattle from one or
more well-known breeders. The host of prize cards pinned on
the boarding on either side of the auctioneer's rostrum, together
with what appear to be two trophies near his feet, reflect the
quality of the Hereford cattle in the ring. So does the good
attendance of farmers and dealers at the sale who have used the
strategically-placed waggons to ensure good vantage points.*

99   Sheep sale, Craven Arms, 1890s
Another well-organised sale, presided over by the south Shropshire firm of Jackson and McCartney (established 1874) whose staff stand in the centre. Large quantities of shiny new metal sheep hurdles have enabled the auction to be transplanted to a parkland setting somewhere in south Shropshire. Potential purchasers line the semi-circle of the main ring at the rear, into which the pens of sheep are driven to come under the hammer. The sheep appear to be Shropshires, a breed which at the close of the nineteenth century had gained a national reputation for their hardiness and productivity.

100 Sheep sale, Craven Arms, late 1890s
The South Shropshire settlement of Craven Arms occupies a textbook market-town site where several valleys converge. In the railway boom of the mid nineteenth century it became an important junction and during the remainder of the century it grew in size and importance. A variety of livestock changed hands in weekly auctions or in the periodic sheep sales like this one in the 1890s. In the background are a number of ricks, with several thatched to keep out the elements.

101 Queens Batch Mill, near Church Stretton, about 1905
*This small mill ground locally-grown corn by using the fast
flowing waters of Marsh Brook as it descended from the nearby
Long Mynd. In the centre of the photograph stand Mr Edwards,
the miller, and his wife, with the mill's three employees on the
right. Despite improved communications and increased
competition the mill remained working until 1951.*

102 Sheep sale, Craven Arms, 1935

The reputation of Craven Arms' annual ewe sales grew steadily throughout the first half of the twentieth century until they gained a prominent position in the national farming calendar. Potential purchasers would journey from throughout the country to attend, and many would use local hotel accommodation on their visit. The marquees on the right of the photograph are likely to have been used by caterers, who would also have been assured of a busy time. Beyond the sheep pens workmen are busy putting the final touches to the Regal cinema. The town itself occupies the land behind the cinema while the railway, bringer of much prosperity to the town, lies behind the photographer.

103 Water mill, Hampton Loade, about 1890
Here the miller and his family pose in front of their brick-built mill in the Severn Valley. This wheel was powered by piped water from the conduit on the right of the photograph. A chamber at the base of the wheel would collect the water as the wheel revolved and return it to stream or river.

104 Wool at Wellington market

Shropshire has long been famous for the quality of wool produced by its native sheep. In the fourteenth century fleeces from sheep in Shropshire were the most highly-prized in the country. Three hundred years later wool from the counties of Herefordshire and Shropshire was considered to be without equal worldwide. The indigenous sheep that supplied such fine wool inhabited several areas of common and heath within the county. From such nimble, hardy but slow-maturing stock evolved the respected Shropshire breed whose breeders led the world in maintaining accurate records of the parentage of each pure-bred animal.

At Wellington market the rolled-up fleeces have arrived from farms in the numbered wool 'sheets'. Although sewn up into closed sacks when they arrived at the market these have since been undone to reveal the quality of the contents.

105 Tractors at Harper Adams College, about 1917

The first surge in the popularity of the farm tractor came during the First World War. (See also plates 109 to 113). Disruptions to the large-scale imports of food meant that home productivity had to increase and the exodus of working horses to assist the army in continental Europe gave the tractor the first chance to prove itself on British soil. American-produced machines predominated as war had severely reduced home production. Styles and designs differed considerably from one maker to another, and practical demonstrations provided the best method of comparison.

The degree to which tractor driving was a female occupation at this time can be gauged by the numbers of Land Army girls in the photograph. They had been brought to the Harper Adams Agricultural College, near Newport, to learn the skills of driving and basic maintenance from a group of male instructors standing on the right of the photograph. The tractors show great variations in appearance, with only the two Fordson 'F's (extreme left and fourth from left) hinting at the shape and simple unitary design of future machines. Between the two Fordsons lie the Titan (left) and Mogul tractors made in the United States by the International Harvester Company. On the right of the photograph are the distinctive Cleveland with its crawler tracks and a heavyweight, three-wheeled Samson.

10 Tractor Power

The first petrol-engined tractor was built in Chicago in 1889 by the Charter Engine Company. Like many machines designed before the First World War it utilised the technology of the steam traction engine and was based upon a heavyweight steel frame. An initial departure from that method of construction was made by an Englishman, Dan Albone of Biggleswade, who produced a versatile lightweight three-wheeler, the Ivel, in 1902. Around 900 of this type were sold between 1902 and 1921, each costing £300.

During the First World War increased demand for tractors encouraged the government purchasing agencies to look to the United States for supplies. Into Britain came new names — the Overtime, and the twin products of the International Harvester Company, the Mogul and the Titan. However, the firm best equipped to supply large numbers of tractors was that of Henry Ford, who applied their car-manufacturing skills to rush through a new concept in tractor design, the Fordson. In this tractor the need for a chassis was removed by using the strong castings of the engine, gearbox and rear axle to give the machine a robust backbone. Following the war other companies followed the Fordson design, but few could match it for reliability or for cost (£260 in 1921) and so even the Austin (at £360) failed to win a sizable market share.

During the 1920s total tractor numbers in the United Kingdom remained stable at around 22,000 with farmers resigned to riding-out difficult economic times with their existing machinery. By the time many were considering a tractor purchase in the 1930s new machines were incorporating several technological advances, including pneumatic tyres, diesel engines, a power take off system for driving stationary machines, and a revised system of directly mounting an implement on the tractor via a three-point linkage.

By the onset of war in 1939 it is estimated that there were about 55,000 tractors in use in Great Britain. Over the next six years the need to increase home production of food led to an unprecedented rise in numbers. By 1945 about 175,000 machines were at work in the countryside, and ninety per cent of British-built ones were Fordsons — still recognisable derivatives of the 1917 Fordson 'F' of the First World War.

106 Tractor at Moreton Corbett, First World War
The tenant of Moreton Corbett farm in the early years or the twentieth century was a Thomas Dale Powell (d. 1935). A successful and progressive farmer, he served as a committee member of several local agricultural societies and sat on the county executive of the National Farmers' Union. He was one of the first in the area to own a motor car and was not slow to see the potential of the internal combustion engine on his 290-acre farm.

Seen here hauling a heavy load of corn is a British-built Saunderson Tractor, with Powell himself at the wheel. Although known to few today, the Saunderson was the best-selling home-produced machine until the advent of the more famous Austin tractor in 1919.

107 Fordson tractor, Cleobury Mortimer, 1936
During the 1930s Fordson tractors became the popular choice of many British farmers. By this time the model F of the First World War had evolved into the much-improved Standard Fordson or Model N, and when production moved from Ireland to Dagenham in 1933 it further strengthened Ford's grip on the tractor market.

It was only during the late 1930s that the use of pneumatic tyres on British-built tractors became popular and the Fordson pictured here still boasts steel rear wheels with metal cleats. These would provide a good grip for fieldwork but would limit the speed and versatility of the tractor. This new Fordson, complete with new plough, is seen at work at Mawley Town farm with Mr Albert Niblett — the farmer and proud owner — standing with his hand on the mudguard.

108 Mechanised harvesting, Moreton Corbett, about 1920
The availability of American-made tractors in Britain increased dramatically after 1917. Thomas Powell presumably took the opportunity to add to his fleet as he is pictured here on a 'Waterloo Boy' — a basic two-cylinder import which ran on paraffin. It appears to be pulling two reaper-binders — one linked to the tractor by a modified wooden hitch (centre) and a second, on the extreme left, attached to the first by a longer pole. With such a work-load the tractor would have replaced between four and six horses, and in theory at least it would also have been able to outlast the combined efforts of its four-footed rivals.

109 Making hen houses, Harper Adams Agricultural College, about 1917
From the earliest stages of the war it was clear that women would have an important role to play as replacements for farmworkers who had joined up. At first training was a problem: some took short courses at agricultural colleges (Harper Adams College running fortnightly courses from the spring of 1915), some trained on farms, and others turned to horticulture. By 1916 women 'of the educated class' were being enrolled in the National Land Service Corps, and in March 1917 the Women's Land Army was set up. Organised by county-based Women's War Agricultural Committees the women assisted in all aspects of farm work including afforestation, cultivation, horticulture, and tractor driving (see plate 105). Here members of the Women's Land Army learn how to make a hen house on a course at the Harper Adams College.

11   The Countryside At War

During the first two years of the First World War food was plentiful: there were bumper harvests, food imports were little affected, and the labour force was maintained. By the end of 1916 the picture had changed, with a poor yield of cereals, the failure of the potato crop, and increased shipping losses from U-boat attacks. Indeed, the situation was critical.

In January 1917 the Board of Agriculture established a Food Production Department to raise production, and to obtain and distribute machinery, labour, and supplies of foodstuffs and fertilizers. The policy was 'Back to the (eighteen-) seventies and better!' War Agricultural Executive Committees, established in each county in 1915 but at first largely ineffectual, were given far-reaching delegated powers. They had the authority to inspect land, issue directions on cultivation, and take possession of badly run farms.

By 1917 one of the biggest problems was the shortage of labour. Many skilled farmworkers had joined the colours, to be replaced by substitutes not always to the farmers' liking. One Shropshire farmer was sent a piano tuner, about whom he complained: 'I could knock nothing in to him!' Frequently more satisfactory was the labour of Land Army Girls, of soldiers on furlough (that is leave for a specific purpose), and of prisoners of war, all of whom made important contributions.

Gradually the picture improved. Despite poor weather, nationally 285,000 acres more were under plough in 1917 than in 1916, an increase not least due to the employment of tractors purchased by the government from America. In Shropshire the best response was from the central parts of the county, while the reaction from rearing and dairying districts like Cleobury Mortimer, Ludlow, and Whitchurch was often slow. Local councils were empowered to create allotments, and almost a million extra were in use by the end of the war. Nevertheless, rationing had to be introduced at the end of 1917, and even basic foodstuffs became short.

The lessons learnt so hard in 1914–18 stood the country in good stead when war threatened once more in the later 1930s. From 1937 stocks of tractors were built up, extra lime and basic slag were applied to the land, and 'War Ag' committees were set up in September 1939. Even so, a formidable task was faced, with over 60 per cent of Britain's foodstuffs coming from abroad.

In Shropshire the ploughing up campaign made good headway: between May 1939 and April 1940 40,000 acres were converted to arable, compared to an additional 27,000 acres in 1917–18. Potato cultivation especially came to the fore, and the war years saw an increase in acreage in the county from 5,000 to 20,000. As in the previous war a comprehensive national policy which included the employment on the land of women, P.O.W.s, and those unable or unwilling to undertake military service, and the speeding up of mechanisation, ensured that the country was kept fed. Rationing there was, but never did the country face the calamity it had in the dark days at the end of 1916.

110 and 111   Threshing, Espley, 1917

Patriotism, the lure of adventure, better wages, and the lack of governmental restrictions all meant that many skilled farmworkers left the land to join up in the first months of the war. As early as June 1915 the Army Council had to agree that furlough, leave of absence, should be given to a limited number of men to work on the harvest, and that no further skilled men would, for the time being, be recruited.

Similar arrangements were made later in the war as well. In 1916 ploughmen were released from the forces to help with the spring cultivation, farmers were allowed to hire horses from military camps, and more men were sent to help with the harvest. Here at Espley, near Cound, soldiers are helping with the threshing, either of the 1916 crop in early 1917, or the 1917 one soon after harvest. The badges and insignia suggest that the three-man team was made up of representatives of the Army Service Corps, the Royal Artillery, and the Royal Welsh Fusiliers.

The threshing set up comprises a steam engine, a Foster threshing machine, and a Ruston stationary baler (see also plate 59), on which the War Department's initials can be seen.

112 Forestry work, Bucknell, about 1917

Women in the Land Army were given a minimum wage together with their clothing and boots. For the most part a tight control seems to have been maintained throughout the war years on who was accepted. What was required, it was felt, was women 'of the better sort', 'sufficiently high in character to make it safe to send them out to live alone on farms or in cottages'. Between 1917 and 1919 nearly half the 43,000 applicants nationally were rejected. Whether or not because of the effects of the careful screening farmers and others seem usually to have quickly overcome any initial scepticism about using such unusual workers. Forestry was one area where women played an important part in the latter stages of the war, and a Women's Forestry Corps, separate from the Land Army, was established. Here at Bucknell women, who look little more than twenty, set to with a two-handed cross-cut saw.

113   Prisoners of war, Shrewsbury, 1919

In Shropshire, as in other counties, prisoners of war were used in the latter stages of the war to supplement the home labour force. Most were drawn from camps at Bromfield and Wem. Seen here, in the garden at Harlescott Farm on the outskirts of Shrewsbury, are Wilhelm and Hermann. Although one cannot be sure from purely pictorial evidence, the several photographs of them in a family photograph album suggest that the pair were healthy, and happy. Although separated from their families, memories of the horrors of the war would still have been fresh, and no doubt they were aware of just how difficult things then were in Germany. They probably stayed at Harlescott until the main repatriation of P.O.W. labourers in the latter part of 1919.

114 School gardening party, Cardington, about 1918
*From the 1880s gardening, dairying and horticulture had begun
to be introduced to the curriculum in the county's schools in a
deliberate attempt to provide relevant vocational training. In
elementary schools gardens were appearing by 1885 and
gradually became more common thereafter. The very serious
food shortages experienced during the First World War
introduced real purpose to the pupils' efforts, and this group
from Cardington school were probably doing their bit for the
war effort. Among those pictured are Stanley Davies, Jack
Davies, and Clem Everall.*

115   Land Army girls, Harper Adams Agricultural College, Second World War
In May 1939, with war once more looming over Europe, preparation for the recruitment of volunteers for the Women's Land Army began. After being provided with a uniform of khaki coat, shirt, breeches and stockings, grey pullover, heavy shoes, and a red and green armband, and if necessary trained, a Land Army girl would either be directly employed on a farm or would join a 'War Ag' gang controlled by the county committee. It may have been into the latter category that these women fell, who are pictured bringing in a load of potatoes. Alternatively, they may have been training on the college farm before receiving a posting.

116 Laying field drains, Coreley, 1941

Between September 1939 and the cessation of recruiting in March 1950, over 200,000 women saw service in the Land Army, 888 of them in Shropshire. As in the First World War theirs was an invaluable contribution, often in very trying circumstances.

Here at Halt Farm, Coreley, field drains are being put in by hand. In Shropshire, as across the rest of the country, drainage systems were all too often neglected in the lean years after the 1870s when the 'Great Depression' settled on agriculture. Many were so clogged with silt that replacement was the only answer, while thousands of acres had never been properly drained in the first place.

As was often the case, romance bloomed on the land, and the Land Army girl ended up marrying her Coreley farmer.

117   Land Army girl, Alcaston, 1943
The young Henry Hand does his bit by helping one of the Land Army girls employed on Alcaston Manor farm, near Church Stretton, with the mucking out. She came with two or three friends from Lancashire — part of a large contingent from that county, mostly mill girls in their early twenties — and was employed directly by the farmer for the standard 48 shillings a week minimum wage. Her leave entitlement would have been seven days a year. Later in the war Italian P.O.W.s replaced the Land Army girls at Alcaston; fifty years on their good nature is still remembered.

118 Timber felling, Buildwas, about 1916

A winter scene, probably during the First World War. Since the late nineteenth century there had been a growing feeling at the national level that a national forestry policy was needed, but by 1914 nothing had been done and ninety per cent of Britain's wood supplies were imported. As in other spheres of rural life heavy wartime demands revealed the desperate need for long-term, government-led reform, policy, and planning. Committee work began in 1916 when the gravity of supply problems suddenly became apparent and came to fruition in 1919 with the establishment under the Forestry Act of the Forestry Commission.

Here the woodmen are beginning to fell a mature oak, using heavy felling axes. They have cleared the base of the trunk of unwanted projections, and are about to begin making the more horizontal cuts to fell the tree. The flagon, and the horn cup held by the left-hand figure, testify to the thirsty nature of the work.

12   Woodland and Timber Industries

For thousands of years, until the advent of mass produced and cheap alternatives in metal and various man-made materials, woodland products were central to many aspects of life. Little of what grew in woods was wasted, and timber, wood, bark, nuts, fungi, and moss were all harvested. By the nineteenth century formal rights of common had been eradicated or had died out in many of Shropshire's ancient woods. Nevertheless, in a good number they survived, and the local inhabitants enjoyed certain customary rights. These, called 'botes' in medieval and later documents — housebote, ploughbote, fencebote, and so on — allowed commoners to take usually carefully defined types and amounts of wood and timber for their own use, and normally went hand-in-hand with the right to graze animals in the wood. What was usually proscribed was the taking of wood for sale or the cutting of 'standards', tall, mature and valuable trees, which belonged to the owner of the wood.

Many landowners, especially in the better-wooded south and west of the county, enjoyed a steady and often considerable income from their woods, and from hedgerow trees, which were also carefully managed. Woods represented an important capital reserve, and in times of financial crisis clear-felling of an estate's woodland (rather than what might be described as a regular culling) could provide a sufficient windfall to pull clear of creditors; such a drastic expedient, however, could only be resorted to once every several generations.

In the later eighteenth and early nineteenth century the county's ancient woods were augmented by the creation of new plantations, principally of deciduous species, on newly-inclosed commons, especially upland ones. In the twentieth century the percentage of coniferous woodland increased considerably as ancient deciduous woods were cleared, and especially through the policies of the Forestry Commission. By 1947 26 per cent of Shropshire's woodlands were coniferous.

Barking

Traditionally there are three ways of tanning, that is turning raw skin, stiff as a board when dry yet soluble in water, into leather, capable of withstanding repeated wetting without its character being altered. Chamoising, where oils and fats are worked into the skin, and tawing, where alum and salt are the preservatives, are both ancient techniques. By far the most common process, however, at least in post-medieval times, was vegetable tanning. Here the skins are soaked in pits containing tanning liquor for several months, even occasionally for as much as three years, until the chemical process of conversion is complete.

While tannin is present in a wide variety of vegetable matter oak bark was the usual source used in British tanneries in the eighteenth, nineteenth and early twentieth centuries. The tanneries consumed vast quantities, both ground to dust and mixed with water to make the tanning liquor for the leaching pits, and also sprinkled directly on hides packed together in layer pits, where the part-tanned hides were placed to allow the slow process of tannin absorption to be completed.

Indeed, so prodigious were the quantities of bark required that it became at the very least an attractive by-product for those landowners possessed of managed woodlands. Nineteenth-century estate accounts from Shropshire indicate that when an oak was felled its bark was worth about a third as much as the timber and wood it yielded. While most bark came from wholesale fellings of oak plantations or coppices the crop was so profitable as never to be neglected, even when only a single tree was to be felled.

119   Loading timber, Bucknell wood, 1895
The photograph shows three medium sized oaks being loaded onto a carriage, the length of which could be adjusted. Horse power was used to raise the timber onto the carriage by means of the pulley and shearlegs. The local term for the job of bringing felled timber down out of the wood to the woodyard was 'tushing', perhaps a variant on the obsolete verb 'tusk' or 'tuft', meaning to drive out game by beating the bushes in a wood. On the hillslope behind the woodmen felled timber lies waiting to be hauled out.

120 Pole hauling, Bucknell wood, 1900
Here B & J. Davies' head waggoner leads a three-horse team out of Bucknell wood with a load of small timber or 'poles'. They are bent or 'waney', and will probably end up as low-grade fencing material or even firewood.

121   Timber hauling, Bucknell, 1914

A large oak being brought into B. & J. Davies' timber yard by 'Boxer', who even on the flat would have found it a heavy load. The timber carriage on which it is carried (seen more clearly in plate 119) had a wheelbase which was adjusted to suit the length of the load. The oak is held steady on it by a 'bracer', a sapling bent across it and secured by chains.

   At the yard the trunk would be sawn into planks which would then be stacked to dry. Much of the oak at this time was sold for fine veneer work. Seen with the load are Fred Munn (on left), his son, and Harry Jones, the waggoner.

122   Timber hauling, Bucknell, 1924
An almost identical view to the last photograph, and ten years on steam haulage has replaced horsepower, at least around Bucknell station yard. The oak is carried on an iron wheeled timber wagon pulled by a 7 hp compound traction engine.

123   Log cutting, Much Wenlock, early twentieth century
The principal landowning family in Much Wenlock in the later nineteenth and earlier twentieth century was the Milnes Gaskells, who bought the Abbey and manor in 1857. The estate was typical of thousands around the country, the family enjoying a comfortable income from a mixture of rents, both urban and rural, and from the direct exploitation of farms and woodlands. Especially in the time of C. G. Milnes Gaskell, owner 1873–1919, house parties were a feature of life at the Abbey, and guests included Thomas Hardy, Henry James, and Philip Webb. The Abbey is a splendid medieval building but cavernous and cold in the winter. Here the estate workmen are gathered together for the autumn log cutting session, using a circular saw driven by a portable steam engine.

124 Gathering firewood, Cardington, about 1903
On most estates tenants seem to have been allowed to take small windfalls and kindling from the landlord's woods, even if earlier rights to take larger wood and timber had been curtailed. Over a year the amount of wood used in fires, ranges, ovens and coppers would be considerable, even in cottages. Also considerable might be the labour involved in gathering it, especially if it were done piecemeal. Such would seem to be the case here, at Oakwood Farm near Cardington, where Eva May Price (later Davies) is shown returning from Oak wood with sticks gathered up in her apron ready to fire the farm's bread oven. By this time the traditional bonnet was old-fashioned for a relatively young woman.

125 Bark peelers near Bucknell, late nineteenth century
The best photographically documented barking centre in Shropshire is Bucknell, which lies on the River Teme in the extreme south-west of the county. Here the traditional barking industry was given a tremendous boost in the early years of the twentieth century by the demands of the Rochdale (later Castleton) firm of John Omerod & Sons Ltd., pulley belt manufacturers.

This photograph is rather earlier than those which follow, and is technically poor. But it is of interest in showing an all-male workforce, albeit one with a wide age spectrum. It is probably significant that it is the most elderly men that are doing the actual stripping, using 'horses', forked branches stuck in the ground, to hold the wood that was being barked. Presumably felling and sawing was left to the younger men.

126 Barking near Buildwas, about 1914–18

Barking was one of those jobs in the agricultural year over which a sense of urgency hung, as the landowner or contractor hurried to get the bark stripped in the weeks in April, May, and early June when it was believed the sap was rising. No great strength was required to prise off the bark, and the agility of youth was a positive boon when a tangled mass of branches had to be dealt with. Thus the casual employment of women and children was common, as here, and in the Nesscliffe Hill area. For women especially the activity was popular, offering an opportunity to boost substantially the family income, relatively good rates of pay being normal. It was also a break from the usual humdrum routine, and even something of a lark with meals being taken communally in the fresh air in a family atmosphere. In the foreground of this photo a kettle and picnic baskets lie next to bonnets, one garlanded with flowers and looking suspiciously like 'best'.

   Behind the baskets is stripped bark, carefully stacked to allow it to dry over two or three weeks to prevent it becoming mildewed. The stacking was probably done by the older women and children, the actual removal being done by the younger women. These hold the tools with which it was done, long barking irons and shorter chisels, driven behind the bark with hammers. The men's job was twofold: to disassemble the tree into workable sections, and to 'ring' the bark with axes and billhooks, cutting round the stem or branch every three feet or so to produce workable lengths for the women to work on.

127 Unloading bark, Bucknell, 1908
Having stood for two or three weeks to dry in the wood the bark was loaded onto specially adapted waggons and hauled back to the rick yard. As the photograph shows, unloading was unceremonious, and as much as anything a testament to the waggon-builder's craft.

128   Ricking bark, Bucknell, 1908
The rick yard was part of the Davies' timber yard, next to the railway line connecting Swansea with Craven Arms. The huge ricks rose only gradually, the bark being carried up onto them on mens' heads in wiskets, locally made baskets of split oak and hazel, filled by women from the heaps dumped out of the waggons. In the centre of this picture stands Omerod's Bucknell agent Mr Pritchard, a local smallholder, who was evidently responsible both for selecting suitable bark and for overseeing its stripping and stacking.

129　A completed bark rick, Bucknell, 1908

As can be grasped from this and the preceding photographs, ricking bark demanded skill and patience. Layers of bark were laid in alternate directions, the complete stack being 'thatched' with more bark to make it watertight. Here, just to make sure, tarpaulins or rick sheets have additionally been employed. In all there might be two or three ricks in the yard, each holding some 250 to 300 tons of bark. As required the bark was taken from the rick, crushed up in a machine similar to a root chopper, bagged, and sent north to Omerod's. Demand could be heavy, and at times the firm was tanning a thousand dozen sheepskins a week.

130 The builder's yard, Lloyney, 1929
A typical small builder's yard, at Lloyney, near Llanfair Waterdine. A wooden-wheeled steam engine is being used to saw boards from locally grown timber, lifted on to the sawbench by shearlegs. Fred Jones, the yard's owner, sits on the sawbench, nearest the engine. The number of wheels in the yard suggests that wheelwrighting may also have gone on there. In the background can be seen the 'Builder's Arms' public house.

131   Joe Lloyd's workshop, Worthen, about 1912

Joe Lloyd (second from left) was a leading light in early twentieth-century Worthen. He was a local councillor, an occasional special constable, post master, coach builder, carpenter, and undertaker, hence his nickname 'the dead man's friend'! Gathered around him are his workmen, with in front a wheelbarrow, part of the Lloyd product range.

Lloyd, remembered as something of a maverick, usually kept a few Shorthorns for pleasure, always as near white as possible. Unlike most of the villagers he was also a Conservative. One morning, during the run up to the 1923 election, Lloyd was infuriated to find that overnight someone had painted his cows red. Furthermore, they had let them out of their field to wander through Worthen, whose villagers were treated to the unlikely spectacle of Lloyd running after his gaudily painted stock bellowing 'come back you radical buggers'!

13 Craftsmen

It was craftsmen's skills, just as much as the food the farmers grew, that made rural communities almost wholly self-sufficient. Countrymen could turn their hand to most things, but some operations were usually left to others, the specialists, whether because a particularly difficult skill was required, or certain specialist tools, or because it was more cost-effective.

If, as has been argued, the earlier nineteenth century saw the average number of specialists in the village increase, the latter part of the century saw their number in decline as the products of the new manufactories were distributed around the country by the railways. Mass produced iron ploughs and rollers, for instance, gradually gained in popularity throughout the early and mid nineteenth century, supplanting the wood and iron ones previously produced by the local village wheelwright and smith.

That gradual contraction in the range of specialist services available continued throughout the period covered in this book and beyond. Nevertheless, the countryside still had a large number of craftsmen. At least in the later nineteenth century most villages of any size usually supported a blacksmith, a wheelwright, and perhaps a carpenter too. Also common were millers, carriers, and builders. Most craftsmen, however, had more than one hat, and even a blacksmith, probably the most common of the specialists in rural Shropshire, was likely to supplement his income by other activities, notably beer selling. Some craft skills, such as clog making, might be practised only seasonally, and still others, such as poaching, on what might best be termed an irregular basis.

Opposite:

132   Cutting thatching spars, Bucknell, about 1900
Until 150 years ago the roofs of Shropshire's houses were predominantly thatched. A survey of Much Wenlock in 1769, for instance, reveals the vast majority of the town's roofs to be of 'straw'. Only a few of the most substantial houses had clay tile roofs, with some others, such as the former prior's lodgings (the modern Wenlock Abbey) having roofs of local stone slates. On the county's meaner cottages and hovels a wider variety of organic materials was employed — bracken, gorse, broom, heather, and almost certainly turf which can make a very effective 'living' roof. In the wetter northern part of the county, especially around the meres and mosses, reeds and sedges were probably used. In the mid nineteenth century, with cheaper methods of mass production and better transport systems, more durable roofing materials became widely available and affordable: flat, clay tiles, many manufactured in the Broseley area, and dark blue or grey Welsh slates. By the end of the century thatched roofs were becoming the exception rather than the norm.

Various materials were used for thatching. Commonest, until the advent of the combine harvester, was the straw left after the cereal harvest, used in 'long straw' thatching. Rye was the thatchers' favourite straw but was in relatively short supply, and accordingly wheat straw was the material most often used. Straw was generally bought from the rick by weight. It was then gathered into bundles or 'yealms' which, tied together with straw rope, were laid directly onto the roof timbers.

About 1900 the Old School House at Bucknell was rethatched by William Trow. As well as large quantities of straw large numbers of timber spars and stays were needed to hold it in place. These might be bought by the thatcher from a woodman such as a hurdle maker, or else he might make his own. Some thatchers even leased a coppice to ensure a good cheap supply of wood. Here Trow is using his spar hook or thatching backer to turn hazel rods into 'buckles', the 28 or 30-inch long split spars used to peg the thatch down. In the background is a bundle of smaller rods which would be used to bind in each course of thatch.

133   Rethatching the Old School House, Bucknell, about 1900

Work is seen here in progress. The new thatch is on the right, the old, mossy thatch to the left. It appears that Trow is putting a layer of new straw onto the old roof, quite a common mid-term rejuvenation, rather than undertaking a comprehensive stripping of the old roof before a fresh start. To the right of Trow the job has been finished and the thatch trimmed up.

   By this date it would have been very unusual to find a smock being worn for work. Nevertheless, it would have been a highly practical overall, sometimes, as in the previous photograph, worn tied up around the waist to give the legs free movement. Also visible in that photograph are Trow's leather knee protectors, an essential part of the thatcher's equipment.

134 The rickyard, Ticklerton, 1891

Long after thatched roofs had become rare there was still heavy seasonal demand for the thatcher's skills in the rickyard, to provide a waterproof covering for straw stacks and hay ricks. Although utilitarian Dutch barns were available from the last quarter of the nineteenth century and tarpaulins from long before, many farms still stored their unthreshed corn, threshed straw, and hay in the historical manner. An element of tradition seems to have been at least partly behind this; the rick building and thatching was one of the high points of the harvest, and well constructed and properly thatched ricks were very much regarded as an indicator of a farmer's efficiency. This is a very neat example, with the thatch continued around the ends of the rick to give added protection.

135 The smithy, Bron y garth, about 1910

Until the mid twentieth century when the working horse was supplanted by the tractor, all villages and many hamlets had a blacksmith.

Local smiths had, in fact, seen much of their traditional work disappear over the previous 150 years. Once they had not only shod horses (and oxen), put iron tyres on wooden wheels, and done running repairs to equipment such as ploughs and harrows, they had also manufactured most of the ironwork found in the countryside. The iron parts of ploughs, tools such as spades, axes, and billhooks, and hundreds of mundane items such as gate hinges, pivots, and bolts, were all made at the local smithy. From the late eighteenth century the necessity for that declined as tools and equipment began to be manufactured by specialist firms and distributed regionally or even nationally.

The Lloyds were smiths here in the late nineteenth century, and it is presumably Frederick Lloyd that is pictured here. While working as a farrier in the army in the First World War one of his eyes was damaged by a flying splinter of metal, and he never thereafter worked as a smith. Bron y garth smithy never reopened, probably as much victim of the declining opportunities outlined above as of the particular personal circumstances of Frederick Lloyd.

136 Gathering fern, Stone Acton, 1891

A straw or reed roof was often too expensive for cottagers, and bracken and fern were among alternative materials used. That, however, was but one use for them. Much, for instance, was burnt for potash in the eighteenth and nineteenth centuries, the ashes being used in glassmaking, soapmaking, and as a detergent. Bracken, bundled up, was even employed (as were faggots) as a primitive land drain.

Almost certainly, however, the load seen here was destined for use as litter in animal pens and sheds. At the time when this photograph was taken 78 per cent of Rushbury parish, of which Stone Acton is an upland township, was grassland. Thus there were many beasts to be overwintered, but relatively little straw was available from cereal crops for bedding. Even in 1990 one or two smallholders on the Clees still used bracken in this way.

Opposite:

137   The old forge and blacksmith's shop, Burwarton, 1930s
As well as there being village smithies many bigger farms had a permanent smithy among the farm buildings. At Burwarton, the centre of Lord Boyne's estate, there could be no doubting where it was housed. Here Mr Bradley of Burwarton Farm positions the foot of his shire cross on the blacksmith's tripod for Mr Wellings (not in photo) to complete the fitting of the shoe.

138   The smithy, Caynham, about 1914
Much of the smith's work was concerned with the repair of the local community's vehicles, from the light traps of the well-to-do to the various types of farm waggon. Here, at the village smithy near Ludlow, new iron tyres are being put on two vehicles by the smith Albert Lane (on right) and three assistants, two of them still in their teens.

Between the second and third workers is a pair of tall lightweight wheels, such as can be seen fitted on the vehicle behind Mr Lane. The other wheels in front of the group comprise the smaller front and larger rear wheels of a heavy waggon — the iron tyre of one of the latter pair can be seen leaning against the left-hand wall of the smithy entrance. Other wheels, or their tyres, can be seen behind Mr Lane.

Opposite:

139 The wheelwright, Aston Eyre, about 1900

Almost certainly the subject of the photograph is William Kidson, the village wheelwright at Aston Eyre at the time the photograph was taken. Behind him hang the tools of his trade, a row of chisels, a brace and bit, and a drawknife, and propped against the bench are some roughed-out spokes. In the foreground stands the wheel he is working on. That has an iron hub, suggesting that it is a commercially manufactured wheel which is in for repair, rather than one of Kidson's own products, likely to have been entirely of wood. Many wheelwrights produced not only wheels but also most other items of timber that a community needed, from window frames to coffins.

140 Village bootmakers, Bucknell, about 1910

Even after the mechanisation of the boot and shoe trade began in the early nineteenth century, and to no small extent its concentration in certain towns and regions, such as Northamptonshire, rural bootmakers survived. Unlike in factories, where the various stages of bootmaking were each performed by a different worker, the rural bootmaker made the whole boot himself. Perversely, in parts of Shropshire work boots (including high-legged waterproof ones) were called 'shoes', with the term 'boot' being reserved for lighter footwear worn on Sundays and on holidays.

In this picture, taken on a summer's day outside 'The Desert' where working boots and shoes were made until 1918, many of the tools of the trade can be seen. Leaning against the bench on the left are clams. Postitioned between the knees the jaws would be used to grip the leather tightly, so leaving the leatherworker's hands free to sew. Also to be seen are several lasts, around which the boots will be assembled. The three men and the apprentice on the right, William Sherwood, each seem to be demonstrating a different part of the bootmaking process, presumably for the photographer's benefit.

141   A clog maker, Hookagate, about 1940

Cheap, mass produced, leather footwear only became available in the later nineteenth century. Until then the main footwear of the working classes, whether in town or countryside, was the clog, a sturdy boot or shoe with a leather upper but a carved wooden sole.

The soles, usually of alder, were fashioned by cloggers working in the wet alder woods themselves, sometimes in gangs. Trees of about 40 to 60 cm diameter were felled and sawn into short lengths, then hewn by axe into rough blocks in a process called 'breaking up'. In this photograph a stock knife is being used to carve the block into the shape of a sole, complete with a notch for the instep. Following this the soles were usually stacked up and left, to allow the wood to season. Later on the finishing of the sole and the attachment of the leather upper might either be done by the clogger himself — who would thus be reckoned a master clogger — or else the soles might be sold on for finishing elsewhere.

During the Second World War a government publicity campaign exhorted the wearing of clogs, available without coupons. But, by then, they were really a thing of the past.

142 Wood turners, Wellington, 1934

The spread of cheap china, tin, and eventually plastic table and domestic wares, and the decline in farm dairying, all contributed to the disappearance of treen, or wooden wares, and the turners that produced them. In the 1940s and 1950s the remaining few and generally elderly turners came to be recognised as the last representatives of an ancient craft and some became quite celebrated. Thus was the case with the turners of Abercuch, in north Pembokeshire, and those of Bucklebury Common, in Berkshire. Shropshire, too, had its wood turners, latterly concentrated in Wellington, a town well known for its wide variety of wood-based crafts and trades in the nineteenth and earlier twentieth centuries and where there had been turners as early as the fourteenth century.

As late as 1940 the town's main manufactory of timber goods, R. Groom, Sons & Co., employed five turners producing a wide range of goods, each from a specific type of wood. Four turners worked in the main factory, but the most skilled of them, John Robert ('Jack') Jordan, worked with his brother Alf in a separate shed in Groom's yard. What set Jack apart was his ability to turn a nest of bowls from a single block of wood. He had the pick of the timber which came into the yard, choosing trunks of a suitable size and grain which were then sawn into short lengths.

It was one of Alf's jobs (here seen on the left, with Jack) to trim the short lengths of trunk, using axe and chopper, into rough blanks ready for Jack to turn. The Jordans' shed is on the left; the floor is strewn with turning waste.

143 Jack Jordan turning, Wellington, about 1940

As with other documented turners, Jack made his own pole lathe, and his own gouges and chisels from old files. The lathe was driven by a belt, seen in the picture, attached below the lathe to a treadle and above it to a springy ash or larch pole. As the treadle was pushed down the lathe chuck turned and the pole bent, spring back up again when the foot was removed. The outside of the nest has already been turned, and Jack is now beginning to cut out the four bowls which will come from the one blank. Probably, as with most vessels and utensils destined for the kitchen and the dairy, it is sycamore that is being used. To his right, in the rack, are various gouges and chisels, and in the foreground a display of finished goods.

Jack continued to work until the early 1940s; his son had declined to follow him as a turner, and Jack refused to teach anyone else. He died, aged eighty-three, in 1953.

Tommy Rogers at IronBridge

144   A coracle builder, Ironbridge, about 1905
By the earlier twentieth century the construction and use of coracles was confined to Wales and the Marches. In the 1920s they were raced at Ironbridge, and in 1936 about eight coracles (each costing about £2.10s) remained in use there. Perhaps best known of the Ironbridge coracle makers in the twentieth century were the successive members of the Rogers family; Eustace Rogers, the grandson of Tom who is pictured here, was still making coracles in 1991, and was reckoned the country's last man to regularly practise the craft.

The framework of the vessel, clearly visible in this photograph, is formed by ash or hazel splints made pliable by soaking, with a gunwale of plaited willow or hazel withies. Willow is also used to make the woven basket-work floor. Originally a single cow hide was used to cover the frame, but from the eighteenth century the usual material was flannel, and later calico or canvas, coated with pitch or tar.

Once the distinctive art of paddling had been mastered a coracle was an excellent riverman's vessel. It was light, portable, and highly manoeuvrable, ideal for nipping across the river, for laying fishing nets, or for discreetly bringing home the proceeds of a night's poaching.